A Classical Chinese Reader

Published by WILD PEONY PTY LTD ACN 002 714 275
PO Box 636 Broadway NSW 2007 Australia
Fax 61 2 9566-1052

International Distribution:
University of Hawaii Press, 2480 Kolowalu Street, Honolulu
Hawaii 96822
Fax 1 808 988-6052

Copyright © Wild Peony 1996

First Published 1996

All rights reserved. No part of this publication may be reproduced, stored in a retrieval system or transmitted in any form or by any means electronic, mechanical, photocopying, recording or otherwise, without the prior permission of the publisher.

ISBN 0 9586526 0 0

Cover photograph: Brick with image of the mythical bird *chu-ch'üeh*, Western Han;
By courtesy of Morning Glory Publishers, Peking.

Printed in Australia by National Capital Printing, Canberra

A Classical Chinese Reader

A. D. Syrokomla-Stefanowska

with the collaboration of

Bi Xiyan

wild peony

We acknowledge the generous support of
The Chiang Ching-kuo Foundation.

Contents

Preface
Abbreviations

Meng-tzu — 1
    IV.B.33 — 2
    I.A.1 — 10
    I.A.3 — 13
    I.A.5 — 22
    From I.A.7 — 26
    I.B.2 — 35
    I.B.6 — 37
    I.B.7 — 39
    I.B.15 — 41
    VI.A.2 — 44
    VI.A.10 — 46
    II.A.6 — 49

Han-fei-tzu — 51
    From "Mr Ho's Jade", c.13 — 52
    From "Criticisms I", c.36 &
        "Outer Collection of Sayings I", c.32 — 55
    From "Five Vermin", c.49 — 57
    From "Two Handles", c.7 — 61

K'ung-tzu Chia-yü — 63
    From "Extending Thought", c.8 — 64

Ta-hsüeh — 67
    From "The Great Learning" — 68

Yen-tzu Ch'un-ch'iu — 70
    From "Inner Chapters, Miscellaneous I", c.6 — 71

Lieh-tzu — 73
    From "The Questions of T'ang", c.5 — 74

Chan-kuo Ts'e — 77
    From "Ch'i Ts'e", 1 — 78
    From "Ch'i Ts'e", 4 — 81
    From "Ch'u Ts'e", 1 — 89

Hsün-tzu — 91
    From "To Encourage Learning", c.1 — 92

Chuang-tzu — 98
    From "The Mountain Tree", c.20 — 99
    From "Hsü Wu-kuei", c.24 & "Autumn Floods", c.17 — 102
    From "Autumn Floods", c.17 — 104

From "Nurturing Life", c.3	106
From "Leisurely Excursion", c.1	109
From "Leisurely Excursion", c.1	114
From "Prising Open Caskets", c.10	116

Kung-sun Lung Tzu   121
   "A White Horse Is Not a Horse"   122

Lun-yü   125
   Selections   126

Lao-tzu   130
   C.2 & c.80   131

Tso-chuan   133
   Duke Hsi 30   134
   Duke Chuang 10   138

Grammatical Notes   140
   The Sentence   141
      The Sentence with a Nominal Predicate   142
      The Interrogative Sentence   143
      The Conditional Sentence   146
      Aspect   147
      Topic   149
      Changes to the Normal Word Order   149
      Ellipsis   151
   Content Words
      Nouns   152
      Pronouns   153
      Verbs   154
      Adjectives   155
   Function Words
      者 *chě*   157
      之 *chīh*   158
      諸 *chū*   159
      而 *érh*   160
      以 *ǐ*   161
      然 *ján*   162
      所 *sǒ*   163
      所以 *sǒ-ǐ*   163
      則 *tsé*   164
      為 *wéi*   164
      為 *wèi*   165
      也 *yěh*   165
      焉 *yēn*   166
      於 *yű*   166

Index   168

Preface

A CLASSICAL CHINESE READER is the result of many years of teaching at the University of Sydney. When I first started teaching, there was little to help the undergraduate student embarking on the study of Classical Chinese. In response to student pleas, I started to provide vocabularies and grammatical notes and finally decided to publish my notes.

In this undertaking I have found the following books particularly useful:
Harold Shadick, *A First Course in Literary Chinese*, Cornell University Press, 1968.
古代漢語 張之強 (ed.), Pei-ching shih-fan ta-hsüeh ch'u-pan-she, Peking, 1984.
古漢語虛詞 楊伯峻, Chung-hua shu-chü, Peking, 1981.
I became aware of *Outline of Classical Chinese Grammar* by Edwin G. Pulleyblank (University of British Columbia Press, 1995) too late to use; I would, however, recommend it to those who want a more detailed outline of Classical Chinese grammar than the one we have provided.

In the Vocabularies, the common Classical Chinese meanings for each word are given; the words are listed only the first time they occur, and the meaning in that passage is marked with the symbol °. Wade-Giles and Pinyin romanization are used in the Vocabularies. In the notes, we have given some historical information that is necessary for the understanding of the passages, as well as explanations of difficult grammatical points and vocabulary; the notes to the early passages are of necessity much more detailed than later ones.

The Grammatical Notes are not meant to be exhaustive. Only the most important points have been covered. We have tried as far as possible to find examples from the passages (page and line numbers are provided); occasionally, however, we have had to look elsewhere.

I should like to thank Bi Xiyan who gave valuable assistance in the last three years. I am also grateful to my colleagues, Associate Professor Mabel Lee, Drs Tony Prince and Lily Lee of the University of Sydney and Dr Lance Eccles of Macquarie University who generously made a gift of their time, reading the manuscript and making suggestions. Finally, I acknowledge with gratitude a grant received from the Chiang Ching-kuo Foundation to support the study of Classical Chinese at the University of Sydney.

Abbreviations

ADJ	Adjective
ADV	Adverb
ADV SUF	Adverbial suffix
CONJ	Conjunction
DEM ADJ	Demonstrative adjective
DEM PRON	Demonstrative pronoun
INT ADJ	Interrogative adjective
INT ADV	Interrogative adverb
INT PART	Interrogative particle
INT PRON	Interrogative pronoun
IO	Indirect object
MW	Measure word
N	Noun
NEG ADV	Negative adverb
NEG PRON	Negative pronoun
NEG V	Negative verb
NUM	Numeral
OBJ	Object
P	Predicate
PART	Particle
PREP	Preposition
PRON	Pronoun
PRON SUF	Pronominal suffix
PW	Place word
REL PRON	Relative pronoun
S	Subject
SUB CONJ	Subordinating conjunction
V AUX	Auxiliary verb
VI	Intransitive verb
VT	Transitive verb

Meng-tzu 孟子

THE dates of Meng-tzu (Mencius) have been reconstructed from the dates of the rulers whom he had met and are generally given as c.372-c.289 B.C. His given name was K'o 軻. Tradition has it that he was a student of Confucius' grandson, Tzu-ssu 子思; this does not seem possible chronologically. However, the teachings of Mencius indicate that he had studied with someone who was well-versed in the thought of Confucius. Mencius travelled from state to state unsuccessfully seeking employment as a counsellor to rulers; finally he returned home and started to teach. The main reason for his lack of success was that during his time, the Warring States period, rulers were interested in state power, in forming alliances and in gaining supremacy; Mencius was seen as too idealistic.

Mencius transmitted the teaching of Confucius: he taught the Confucian virtues, the most important of which was goodness (*jen* 仁), he supported the same method of government by moral virtue.

The *Meng-tzu* is a record of conversations between Mencius and his contemporaries—rulers, disciples, friends and adversaries—and of his sayings. The prose style is lucid and lively.

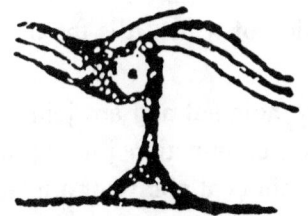

孟子 IV.B.33

齊人有一妻一妾而₁處室₂者₃，其良人出，則₄必饜酒肉而後₅反。其妻問所₆與飲食者，則盡富貴也。其妻告其妾曰："良人出，則必饜酒肉而後反；問其與飲食者，盡富貴也，而未嘗有顯者來，吾將瞷良人之所之₇也。"

---

1 而 is a conjunction used to connect verbs, verbal clauses and adverbs to verbs. Often it joins two clauses in which the verb in the second clause is modified by the first clause showing the way something is done or the sequence in which it is done. In this sentence 一妻一妾 shows the circumstances under which the man lived in the house and may be translated "with a wife and a concubine".

2 處室, to live in a house. The preposition 於 is often omitted.

3 者 is a pronominal suffix used to convert an adjective, verb or a predicate into a nominal clause: one who (is or does), those who (are or do), that which (is or does). The preceding clause, verb or adjective qualifies the person, thing or event represented by 者. 有 indicates existence. 齊人有… 者 means: Among the men of Ch'i there was one who….

4 則 often gives a conditional or temporal meaning to the preceding clause: A 則 B = if or when A then B. The first clause sets out the circumstances under which the second clause is true. This sentence may be best rendered: whenever A then B.

5 而後, and afterwards, and then; implies that what occurs in the second clause can occur only after the action of the first clause has been completed.

6 所 is a relative pronoun indicating a person, event or thing; it always stands before the verb or preposition of which it is the object. 所與… 者, the ones with whom.

7 之所之: 所 phrases are nominal and are joined to the noun by 之, which in this case is a subordinating conjunction joining attribute to noun to form the possessive case, a complex nominal phrase or a relative clause. Here the resulting nominal clause 良人之所之 is the object of 瞷. The second 之 is a verb.

蚤起，施從良人之所之，遍國中無與¹立談者²。卒之東郭墦閒，之祭者，乞其餘；不足，又顧而之他 — 此其為饜足之道也³。

其妻歸，告其妾，曰："良人者，所仰望而終身⁴也，今若此 —"與其妾訕其良人，而相泣⁵於中庭，而良人未之知⁶也，施施從外來，驕⁷其妻妾。

由君子觀之，則人之所以求富貴利達者，其妻妾不羞也，而不相泣者，幾希矣⁸。

---

1 與 implies 與之, with him.
2 無… 者 is the negative of 有… 者, there was no-one who….
3 此… 也: the commonest use of 也 is as a marker of a nominal predicate: A B 也 or A 者 B 也 = A is B. In this sentence 此 is the subject and 其為饜足之道也 is the nominal predicate.
4 After the 而, 終身 functions as a verb and means "to rely on (someone) the whole of one's life".
5 相泣 here implies 相與泣, with each other (together) wept.
6 未之知: in negative sentences the pronoun object 之 stands before the verb.
7 Preposition 於 omitted after 驕.
8 人之所以求富貴利達者，其妻妾不羞，而不相泣者，幾希矣: in this sentence the first 者 and the 也 serve as markers of a pause. 人… 泣者 is the whole subject and 幾希 is the predicate.

MENG-TZU IV.B.33

Vocabulary

孟	mèng	N °a surname ADJ first, eldest
子	tzǔ/zǐ	N son, child; °master; form of address: you, Sir
齊	ch'í/qí	N °one of the ancient Chinese states ADJ even, equal VT make even; keep in order
人	jén/rén	N person, man
有	yǔ/yǒu	VT have, °there is/are
妻	ch'ī/qī	N °wife VT marry a woman off
妾	ch'ièh/qiè	N °concubine; deferential term often used by a woman to refer to herself
而	érh/ér	CONJ °and, and also, but PRON you
處	ch'ǔ/chǔ	VI °live, dwell, stay VT manage, deal with; sentence, judge
	ch'ù/chù	N place
室	shìh/shì	N °house, room; family, home, wife; tomb; sheath
者	chě/zhě	PRON SUF one who (is or does), those who (are or do), that which (is or does)
其	ch'í/qí	PRON third person pronoun possessive: his, hers, its, °their PART used as an initial particle to give mild imperative mood to sentence: "let us", "may you"; to intensify exclamatory sentence; or to give hypothetical force to sentence DEM PRON that, this, the
良	liáng	ADJ good, pure, capable ADV very, really
良人	liáng-jén/ liángrén	N °husband; beautiful woman; upright person
出	ch'ū/chū	VI come out, °go out, appear VT produce, bring forth, issue
則	tsé/zé	SUB CONJ °then; thus
必	pì/bì	ADV necessarily, °certainly, must
饜	yèn/yàn	VT °be satisfied with VI be full of, be satisfied
酒	chiǔ/jiǔ	N alcoholic drink
肉	jòu/ròu	N °meat, flesh; pulp

後	hòu	ADV later, °afterwards ADJ later, rear VT put last N posterity, rear
反	fǎn	VI turn; restore; °return (used for 返) VT return; turn around; oppose, rebel ADV inside out; on the contrary
問	wèn	VT °ask; investigate; inquire about N order
所	sŏ/suŏ	PRON that which, what is, place where
與	yǔ/yǔ	CONJ and VT give to; associate with PREP °together with, with, for
	yǘ/yú	PART final interrogative particle, often used in rhetorical questions expecting an affirmative answer, usually written 歟
	yù/yù	VI share in, take part in
飲	yǐn	VT & VI °drink; tolerate; swallow N drink
	yìn	VT give to drink, water (e.g., a horse or cattle)
食	shíh/shí	VI °eat N food VT eat
	ssù/sì	VT feed
盡	chìn/jìn	ADV fully, entirely, °all VT use up, exhaust
富	fù	N °the rich, riches ADJ rich, wealthy
貴	kuèi/guì	N honours; °the noble, the honourable, high position ADJ noble; precious
也	yěh/yě	PART final particle used as a marker at the end of a clause
告	kào/gào	VT report; °tell, inform; ask; lay an accusation
曰	yüēh/yuē	VT °introduces direct quotation: says, said; be called
未	wèi	NEG ADV not yet, °never N the eighth of the twelve earthly branches
嘗	ch'áng/cháng	VT taste; try; experience ADV °once; in the past
顯	hsiěn/xiǎn	ADJ apparent, obvious; °illustrious VI appear

MENG-TZU IV.B.33

來	lái	VI come
吾	wú	PRON °I, my, me
將	chiāng/jiāng	ADV indicates incipient action: be about to, will have, °intend, plan to; indicates approximate number: nearly, almost CONJ indicates a choice: or VT take; lead, command
	chiàng/jiàng	N leader, general
	ch'iāng/qiāng	V AUX be willing to; wish
瞷	chièn/jiàn	VI °spy on, peep at
之	chīh/zhī	SUB CONJ of, ...'s PRON OBJ him, her, it, them VT go to DEM PRON this, that
蚤	tsǎo/zǎo	ADJ & ADV early, in the morning (used for 早)
起	ch'ǐ/qǐ	VI °rise, start VT rise from, start
施	í/yí	ADV (to walk) obliquely; °(to follow) a winding, roundabout path (used for 迤)
從	ts'úng/cóng	VT °follow, accompany; devote oneself to PREP from
	tsùng/zòng	N follower, attendant
遍	pièn/biàn	ADV everywhere
國	kuó/guó	N country, state, fief, °capital city
中	chūng/zhōng	N centre, middle ADJ middle PW °in, among, in the middle of
	chùng/zhòng	VT hit target, fit exactly VI be affected by
無	wú	NEG V negative of 有: not to have, °there is not, lack NEG ADV do not
立	lì	VI & VT °stand; erect; establish; exist ADJ upright, immediate
談	t'án/tán	VI °talk, chat; discuss N conversation
卒	tsú/zú	ADV °finally ADJ dead N soldier; pawn
東	tūng/dōng	N east; host, master ADJ °eastern

郭	kuō/guō	N °outer city, outer wall; outer case
墦	fán	N grave
閒	chiēn/jiān	PW °among, between (also written 間) N crevice, space between
	hsién/xián	N leisure ADJ light, idle; free, untrammelled ADV idly
祭	chì/jì	VI °hold a memorial ceremony, sacrifice to (ancestors or spirits) N sacrifice
乞	ch'ǐ/qǐ	VT °beg, ask
餘	yǘ/yú	ADJ spare, remaining N °leftovers, surplus, remainder ADV beyond, after
不	pù/bù	NEG ADV not, does not
足	tsú/zú	N foot V AUX be sufficient to, be adequate to ADJ enough, sufficient VI °be sufficient VT make sufficient
又	yù/yòu	ADV °again CONJ and, also; further, in addition
顧	kù/gù	VI & VT °look around, look back; look after (someone), care for; visit
他	t'ā/tā	PRON other, others, °another ADJ other, another
此	tz'ǔ/cǐ	DEM PRON °this ADV here
為	wéi	VT consider as, function as, do, make, °become
	wèi	VT act on behalf of PREP for the sake of, for, by
道	tào/dào	N °the way, way of life or conduct; path, road VT speak of
	tǎo/dǎo	VT lead, guide
歸	kuēi/guī	VT go back to, return; give back to VI go home, °return; come together; converge on; marry off a daughter N final resting-place, destination
仰	yǎng	VI look up VT admire, °respect

望	wàng	VI gaze into the distance VT °hope, expect, long for; gaze at something in the distance N full moon, the 15th day of the lunar month
仰望	yǎng-wàng	VT to respectfully seek guidance or help from
終	chūng/zhōng	N end, finish, death ADJ °whole; final ADV in the end, finally VT bring to an end VI come to an end, die
身	shēn	N body, oneself; °life; one's moral character and conduct ADV in person
今	chīn/jīn	ADV °now ADJ present N the present
若	jò/ruò	PREP like, seem, as for CONJ if PRON you DEM PRON this VT resemble, °be like, be equal to
訕	shàn	VT °abuse, slander
相	hsiāng/xiāng	ADV °mutually, each other. Indicates action by one person affecting another, or action affecting both parties simultaneously, 相見 can mean, depending on context, we see each other, I see him/her or he/she sees me.
	hsiàng/xiàng	N high minister; appearance VT look at, examine; act as adviser to, assist
泣	ch'ì/qì	VI °weep N tears
於	yǘ/yú	PREP at, °in, on, by, than, etc.
庭	t'íng/tíng	N °front courtyard; hall; court
知	chīh/zhī	VT °know, realize, be aware; inform, administer ADJ intimate
	chìh/zhì	N knowledge
施	shīh/shī	VT bestow, grant; exhibit, display; apply, do
施施	shīh-shīh/shīshī	ADV °smugly, complacently (also pronounced í-í/yíyí)
外	wài	N °outside ADJ outer
驕	chiāo/jiāo	VI °be arrogant, act haughtily ADJ haughty

由	yú/yóu	CONJ like (used for 猶) VT follow, act in accordance with PREP °from, because of N cause, source
君	chūn/jūn	N lord, ruler; a respectful form of address for both men and women
君子	chūn-tzǔ/jūnzǐ	N °gentleman, a man of noble character; form of address used by inferior to superior, wife to husband
觀	kuān/guān	VT °observe, view; show
	kuàn/guàn	N gate tower; Taoist temple
以	ǐ/yǐ	N means VT take, use, consider PREP °by means of, with, because, by, through, on account of, according to CONJ in order to, so as to; and
所以	sǒ-ǐ/suǒyǐ	PRON + PREP that with which, the reason why, °the means by which
求	ch'iú/qiú	VT °seek; beg, request, demand VI strive for N demand, need; end
利	lì	N °benefit, profit; interest VT benefit, do good to ADJ favourable; sharp ADV smoothly, successfully
達	tá/dá	VI get to, penetrate, break through, reach; succeed VT understand; express ADJ illustrious, successful; fluent; smooth; intelligent N °success
羞	hsiū/xiū	N good food, delicacy; shame VT & VI °be ashamed or embarrassed, feel ashamed of
幾	chǐ/jǐ	ADJ few, several; how much or many
	chī/jī	ADV °almost, nearly
希	hsī/xī	ADJ scarce, °rare, few
幾希	chī-hsī/jīxī	ADJ very few
矣	ǐ/yǐ	PART used in final position to indicate completed action, a new situation or a mild command

孟子 I.A.1

孟子見梁惠王1。王曰："叟！不遠2千里而來，亦將有以3利吾國乎？"

孟子對曰："王！何必曰利？亦有仁義而已矣4。王曰：'何以5利吾國？'大夫6曰：'何以利吾家？'士庶人曰：'何以利吾身？'上下交征利而國危矣。萬乘7之國，弒其君者，必千乘之家。千乘之國，弒其君者，必百乘之家。萬取千焉8，千取百焉，不為不多矣。苟為9後義而先利，不奪不饜10。未有仁11而遺其親者也，未有義而後其君者也。王亦曰仁義而已矣，何必曰利？"

---

1 梁惠王, King Hui of Liang (r. 369-335 B.C.). Hui was his posthumous or temple name, the name used whenever a ruler was referred to after his death. Liang was the name used for the state of Wei 魏 after 362 B.C.

2 遠: when used as a transitive verb an adjective has a putative or causative meaning, i.e., consider or cause to be far.

3 有以, to have that with which to; this is probably a contraction of 有所以.

4 而已矣 is a final phrase meaning "and that is all".

5 何以 is an INT PRON + PREP: by what means, how. Interrogative pronouns are generally placed in front of the verb or preposition of which they are the object.

6 *Tài-fū*, 大夫, grand master, great officer; during the Chou dynasty the second highest category of officials.

7 乘 is a conventional way to refer to the strength of a state or a fief; a 10,000 war-chariot state was a large and powerful one.

8 焉 is a fusion of 於之, PREP + PRON OBJ. The pronoun object refers to 萬 which has been placed in the position of a topical subject.

9 苟為 means "if", it is an idiomatic expression.

10 不奪不饜: symmetrical clauses may express a conditional or a temporal relationship between two clauses: if... then..., whenever... then.... Such sentences refer to universal truths.

11 仁 in this clause and 義 in the next are given a verbal meaning by the 而 which follows.

Vocabulary

見	chièn/jiàn	VT °see, have audience with V AUX indicates the passive voice
	hsièn/xiàn	VI appear (used for 現)
梁	liáng	N °name of a state; bridge, beam, dam
惠	huì	N °a proper name; kindness, favour ADJ kind
王	wáng	N °king, prince
	wàng	VI rule, be a king
叟	sǒu	N old man; °polite form of address: Reverend Sir
遠	yüǎn/yuǎn	ADJ °far, distant
千	ch'iēn/qiān	NUM one thousand
里	lǐ	N °a measure of distance, approx. 500 metres; village, hamlet
亦	ì/yì	ADV also, too, only; °surely, indeed CONJ and also, but also, besides, still, too
乎	hū	PART °final interrogative or exclamatory particle PREP used like 於
對	tuì/duì	VI °reply, answer VT agree, match
何	hó/hé	INT ADV °why, how INT ADJ what, what kind INT PRON what, where
仁	jén/rén	N goodness, benevolence
義	ì/yì	N °righteousness, duty, just; meaning ADJ fair, high-principled
已	ǐ/yǐ	VI °end VT bring to an end; dismiss ADV already
大	tà/dà	ADJ °great, big ADV greatly
	tài/dài	ADJ great (this pronunciation is used in titles, e.g., 大王 and 大夫)
	t'ài/tài	ADJ used for 太
夫	fū	N °man, male
	fú	DEM ADJ this, that PART used to introduce an argument or a narration: now as regards
家	chiā/jiā	N °household, family, home
士	shìh/shì	N °officer, scholar

庶	shù	ADJ many, °belonging to the masses ADV nearly; perhaps
庶人	shù-jén/shùrén	N commoners
上	shàng	N °superior, top, emperor VI rise, go up VT present to superiors; mount ADJ upper, superior; previous
下	hsià/xià	N °inferior, bottom VI descend, go down VT send down (e.g. an order); dismount from ADJ lower, inferior
交	chiāo/jiāo	ADV °mutually; together VT join, have relations with, exchange; interlock
征	chēng/zhēng	VT °strive for; attack (in just cause), go on military campaign
危	wēi	VI °be in danger VT endanger ADJ dangerous; lofty
萬	wàn	NUM ten thousand
乘	shèng	N °war chariot drawn by four horses
	ch'éng/chéng	VT mount, drive, ride on; avail of, take advantage of
弒	shìh/shì	VT assassinate (a superior)
百	păi/băi	NUM one hundred
取	ch'ǔ/qǔ	VT °take, seize; choose, get
焉	yēn/yān	PART °a fusion of PREP 於 + PRON OBJ 之: in, at, from etc. + him, her, it, them INT PRON where, how, who, what
多	tō/duō	ADJ °much, many ADV mostly VI increase
苟	kŏu/gŏu	CONJ °if ADV carelessly
先	hsiēn/xiān	VT °put first; precede ADV before, first ADJ first; former
奪	tó/duó	VT snatch
遺	í/yí	VT °neglect; leave behind, bequeath, hand down
	wèi	VT present
親	ch'īn/qīn	N °parents, close relative ADJ close, intimate ADV in person VT feel close to, love

孟子 I.A.3

　梁惠王曰："寡人1之於2國也，盡心焉耳矣。河內3凶，則移其民於河東4，移其粟於河內。河東凶亦然。察鄰國之政，無如寡人之用心者5。鄰國之民不加少，寡人之民不加多，何也6？"

　孟子對曰："王好戰。請以戰喻。填然7鼓8之，兵刃既接，棄甲曳兵而走。或9百步而後止，或五十步而後止。以五十步笑百步，則何如10？"

　曰："不可。直不百步耳，是亦走也11。"

1　寡人 is the conventional way for a ruler to refer to himself.
2　之於 used between two nouns means "relationship to, attitude to". The clause 寡人之於國也 is nominal and makes the subject 寡人 and the object 國 the topic of the sentence. The object is resumed by 焉, to it, i.e., to my country.
3　河內: area on the north bank of the Yellow River in modern Honan 河南.
4　河東: area of Wei lying east of the Yellow River in modern Shansi 山西.
5　無如… 者, there is no-one like…, no-one equals…. In 寡人之用心, 之 transforms S + P into a nominal clause which is the object of 如.
6　X, 何也, why is it that X (lit., X is why). This equational construction is a common way of asking a question.
7　然 is an adverbial suffix: -ly.
8　鼓: a noun used as a transitive verb may indicate an action performed by whatever the noun refers to, here, use a drum to arouse them to action.
9　或… 或…, some… others….
10　何如 is a phrase used when asking questions about a proposed course of action, nature of an event or opinion on something: what would you think, what about it.
11　是亦走也 is an equational sentence: 是 (DEM PRON) is the subject and 走 (used as a N) is the nominal predicate.

曰：＂王如¹知此，則無望民之多於鄰國²也。

＂不違農時³，穀不可勝食也；數罟不入洿池，魚鱉不可勝食也；斧斤以時⁴入山林，材木不可勝用也。穀與⁵魚鱉不可勝食，材木不可勝用，是使民養生喪死無憾⁶也。養生喪死無憾，王道⁷之始也。

＂五畝之宅，樹之以桑，五十者⁸可以衣帛矣。雞豚狗彘之畜，無失其時，七十者可以食肉矣。百畝之田，勿奪其時，數口之家可以無飢矣。謹庠序之教，申之以孝悌之義，頒白者不負戴於道路矣。七十者衣帛食肉，黎民不飢不寒，然而不王⁹者，未之有也。

---

1 如, if, often follows the subject of a conditional clause, as it does here.
2 民之多於鄰國 is a S + P object of 望 made nominal by inserting 之 after the subject. This is a common construction when the subject of the object clause is not the same as the subject of the sentence, e.g., after verbs of knowing, seeing, hearing, hoping, etc. 於 after an adjective makes the adjective comparative: 多於 more numerous than.
3 不違農時…: this sentence and the following two are conditional; context alone suggests this.
4 以時, according to the time, i.e., at the right time or season.
5 與 is used as a conjunction between nouns. Here it joins two groups of things.
6 養生喪死無憾: the main verb is 無 and the first four characters modify it.
7 王道, kingly or royal way. Chinese thought speaks of three ways: the sovereign way 帝道, i.e., the government of the mythical sage rulers whose rule was believed to have resulted in a utopia; the royal way 王道, i.e., the government of just kings who ruled according to the rites; and the way of the overlords 霸道 (pà-tào) i.e., the rule of the most powerful of the feudal lords who were interested only in power and wealth.
8 五十者 indicates age: the ones who are fifty years old.
9 王 is a verb meaning "to be a king, to rule". In Confucian thought it implies to be a good king, to rule humanely, to behave as a ruler ought to behave.

"狗彘食人食而不知檢,塗有餓莩而不知發;人死,則曰,'非¹我也,歲也。'是何異於刺人而殺之,曰,'非我也,兵也。'王無罪歲,斯天下之民至焉。"

---

1 非 is the negative verb used to negate nominal predicates: A 非 B 也 = A is not B. In sentences such as "it is/is not I" where the English "it" refers to the subject of thought or inquiry, the subject is omitted.

Vocabulary

寡	kuǎ/guǎ	ADJ few, solitary N widow
心	hsīn/xīn	N heart, mind
耳	ěrh/ěr	PART °a fusion of 而 + 已: and that is all N ear
河	hó/hé	N river; °the Yellow River
內	nèi	N inside ADJ inner ADV within, inside
凶	hsiūng/xiōng	VI °suffer calamity, be in distress ADJ disastrous, unlucky
移	í/yí	VT °transfer, move, change VI move, change
民	mín	N °the people, subjects
粟	sù	N grain
然	ján/rán	ADJ (it is) so, thus, (to be) so, °like this CONJ but, however ADV SUF -like, -ly VI burn (used for 燃)
察	ch'á/chá	VT examine
鄰	lín	ADJ °neighbouring N neighbour, neighbourhood
政	chèng/zhèng	N °administration, government
如	jú/rú	VT °be like, resemble, be equal; go to PREP like, as if, as CONJ if
用	yùng/yòng	VT °use, employ PREP by means of
加	chiā/jiā	ADV °increasingly, more VT put on top, add
少	shǎo	VI °become fewer ADJ few
好	hào	VT °like, be fond of
	hǎo	ADJ good, fine
戰	chàn/zhàn	VI fight a battle N °battle, war
請	ch'ǐng/qǐng	ADV please VT ask for, invite V AUX ask permission, °permit (me), allow (me) to

喻	yü/yù	VI °illustrate VT enlighten, understand
填	t'ién/tián	ADJ °booming, rumbling (of a drum) VT fill
鼓	kǔ/gǔ	VT °drum, arouse (to action) N drum
兵	pīng/bīng	N °weapon, soldier
刃	jèn/rèn	N °edge or tip of sword, blade VT kill with sword
既	chì/jì	ADV °already SUB CONJ since, when VI end, finish
接	chiēh/jiē	VI °be joined VT come in contact with, join, meet, welcome
棄	ch'ì/qì	VT °abandon, reject, discard
甲	chiǎ/jiǎ	N °armour, shell; first of the 10 heavenly stems
曳	yèh/yè	VT °drag, trail
走	tsǒu/zǒu	VI °flee, run
或	huò	PRON someone, °some ADV perhaps, possibly, in some cases
步	pù/bù	N °step, pace VT follow in footsteps
止	chǐh/zhǐ	VI & VT °stop N foot (used for 趾) ADV only
笑	hsiào/xiào	VT °laugh at VI laugh, smile
可	k'ǒ/kě	ADJ °permissible V AUX may, can
直	chíh/zhí	ADV °merely, only ADJ straight, upright
是	shìh/shì	DEM PRON °this N right
違	wéi	VT °go against, oppose; avoid
農	núng/nóng	N farming, agriculture
時	shíh/shí	N °season, time ADV at that time, at times
穀	kǔ/gǔ	N grain
勝	shēng	ADV °fully, exhaustively VT bear, endure

	shèng	VT overcome, surpass VI win a victory ADJ beautiful (of scenic place, etc.)
數	ts'ù/cù	ADJ °fine, close
	shù	ADJ several, a number of N amount; destiny, fate
	shǔ	VT count
	shuò	ADV frequently
罟	kǔ/gǔ	N net
入	jù/rù	VT cause to enter, admit VI °enter N income
洿	wū	N °pool, stagnant water ADJ dirty
池	ch'íh/chí	N pool
魚	yǘ/yú	N fish
鱉	pīeh/biē	N turtle
斧	fǔ	N axe
斤	chīn/jīn	N °axe; a weight: one catty
山	shān	N mountain
林	lín	N forest
材	ts'ái/cái	N °timber, material; ability
木	mù	N °tree, wood
使	shǐh/shǐ	VT °allow, cause, order, commission, employ; serve as an envoy N envoy CONJ if, supposing
養	yǎng	VT °support, nourish, raise, rear
生	shēng	N °the living, life VI be born, arise, grow, live VT produce ADJ living, raw, fresh
喪	sāng	VT °mourn N funeral
	sàng	VT lose; die, destroy
死	ssǔ/sǐ	N °the dead VI die
憾	hàn	N °resentment, dissatisfaction; regret

始	shǐh/shǐ	N °the beginning VI begin ADJ first ADV in the beginning; just
畝	mǔ	N a land measure; field
宅	chái/zhái	N °house, residence VT dwell in, reside in
樹	shù	VT °plant, establish N tree
桑	sāng	N mulberry
衣	ì/yì	VT °wear
	ī/yī	N clothes, jacket
帛	pó/bó	N silk
雞	chī/jī	N chicken
豚	t'ún/tún	N sucking pig
狗	kǒu/gǒu	N dog
彘	chìh/zhì	N pig
畜	hsǜ/xù	N °breeding, rearing VT rear, breed, support
	ch'ù/chù	N domestic animals
失	shīh/shī	VT lose; °neglect VI fail, err
田	t'ién/tián	N °cultivated land, field VI hunt (used for 畋)
勿	wù	NEG ADV do not
口	k'ǒu/kǒu	N mouth; opening; °number of people in a family
飢	chī/jī	N °hunger, famine VI be hungry ADJ hungry
謹	chǐn/jǐn	VT °pay attention to ADJ attentive, respectful
庠	hsiáng/xiáng	N school
序	hsǜ/xù	N °school; order; preface VT arrange in order
庠序	hsiáng-hsǜ/ xiángxù	N school
教	chiào/jiào	N °teaching

	chiāo/jiāo	VT teach VT cause
申	shēn	VT extend, stretch; repeat; state, notify; °repeatedly instruct N ninth of the twelve earthly branches
孝	hsiào/xiào	N °filial piety ADJ filial
悌	t'ì/tì	N fraternal piety
頒	pān/bān	ADJ °variegated (also written 斑) VT proclaim
白	pái/bái	ADJ white
頒白	pān-pái/bānbái	ADJ grey (of hair)
負	fù	VI & VT °carry on back; neglect; turn back on, stand with back to VI be defeated N defeat, failure
戴	tài/dài	VI & VT °carry on head, support; hold in high esteem
路	lù	N road
黎	lí	ADJ numerous; black, black-haired; °the common people
寒	hán	ADJ cold
檢	chiěn/jiǎn	VT control, restrict; examine; °store, accumulate (used for 斂) N rule, law
塗	t'ú/tú	N °road, mud
餓	ò/è	ADJ starving
莩	p'iǎo/piǎo	VI die of starvation (used for 殍)
發	fā	VT issue, promulgate, °distribute, send forth; open VI start out, set forth
非	fēi	NEG V °is not, are not N & ADJ wrong SUB CONJ unless, if not... then VT deny, condemn
我	wǒ	PRON °I, we
歲	suì	N year, age (used to count a person's age), °harvest
異	ì/yì	ADJ different; strange VI °be different, be surprised VT consider strange

刺	tz'ù/cì	VT °stab, pierce; criticize N thorn
殺	shā	VT °kill; destroy, ruin VI decline
	shài	VT decrease
	sà	ADJ light, pale (of colour)
罪	tsuì/zuì	N crime, guilt VT °blame, condemn
斯	ssū/sī	DEM ADJ & PRON this CONJ °then
天	t'iēn/tiān	N heaven, nature
天下	t'iēn-hsià/ tiānxià	N the world, the empire (i.e., everything under heaven)
至	chìh/zhì	VI °come, reach, be perfect N extreme, highest point, perfection ADV extremely, perfectly ADJ ultimate

孟子 I.A.5

梁惠王曰："晉[1]國，天下莫強焉[2]，叟之所知也。及[3]寡人之身，東敗於[4]齊，長子死焉。西喪地於秦七百里；南辱於楚。寡人恥之，願比死者壹洒之，如之何[5]則可？"

孟子對曰："地方[6]百里而可以王。王如施仁政於民，省刑罰，薄稅斂，深耕易耨；壯者以暇日修其孝悌忠信，入[7]以事其父兄，出以事其長上，可使制梃以撻秦楚之堅甲利兵矣。

"彼奪其民時，使不得耕耨以養其父母。父母凍餓，兄弟妻子離散。彼陷溺其民，王往而征之，夫誰與王敵？故曰：'仁者無敵。'王請勿[8]疑！"

---

1 晉 was the most powerful state in the sixth century B.C. In 403 B.C. it was divided into three states, one of which was Wei 魏 or as it was called after 362 B.C. 梁. Here the king is referring to Wei.
2 焉 is a fusion of 於之, after an adjective: more... than it.
3 及 is used as a preposition to introduce a temporal clause: "up to my person", i.e., "during my lifetime" and in this example "while I have been on the throne".
4 於 introduces the agent of a passive verb: by.
5 如之何 is an idiomatic expression meaning "how is one to achieve it", "what is one to do about it". In the phrase 如 is a verb meaning "to be like", 之 is a pronoun object and 何 is an interrogative pronoun.
6 方, square, refers to 百里 a hundred *li* square.
7 入… 出…, at home... (away from home=) in office....
8 勿 at times, as here, implies 勿之.

Vocabulary

晉	chìn/jìn	N name of one of the Chinese states
莫	mò	NEG PRON °none, no-one, nobody, nothing NEG ADV do not
強	ch'iáng/qiáng	ADJ °strong, violent VT strengthen
	ch'iăng/qiăng	VT force, compel
及	chí/jí	VT come up to, reach PREP °up to, till; when CONJ and, and also
敗	pài/bài	VI °be defeated VT ruin, defeat
長	chăng/zhăng	ADJ senior, °eldest VI grow tall N elder, senior
	ch'áng/cháng	ADJ long, tall; far-reaching ADV for a long time, always
西	hsī/xī	N west
地	tì/dì	N the earth, region, °territory, place
秦	ch'ín/qín	N name of one of the Chinese states
南	nán	N south
辱	jŭ/rŭ	VT disgrace, put to shame VI °be disgraced
楚	ch'ŭ/chŭ	N °name of one of the Chinese states; rod; pain ADJ sharp; clear; beautiful
恥	ch'ĭh/chĭ	VT °be ashamed of N shame
願	yüàn/yuàn	VT think of, long for, desire V AUX °wish to, be willing to
比	pĭ/bĭ	PREP °on behalf of, for, up to VT come up to, put side by side, associate with, be near; compare ADJ equal ADV recently, frequently; when
壹	ī/yī	NUM one (same as 一) ADV °completely
洒	hsĭ/xĭ	VT °wipe away
	să	VT sprinkle
方	fāng	N °square; region; direction; method VI form a square ADJ square; just then, just now

省	shěng	VT °diminish ADJ frugal
	hsǐng/xǐng	VT examine
刑	hsíng/xíng	N °punishment, law; model VT punish VI be a model
罰	fá	N °punishment VT punish
薄	pó/bó	VT °make light; reach to, approach; regard with contempt ADJ light, poor, mean, thin
稅	shuì	N °taxes, revenue
斂	liěn/liǎn	N °taxes, revenue
	lièn/liàn	VT gather, collect
深	shēn	ADJ deep, profound ADV °deeply
耕	kēng/gēng	VT & VI plough
易	ì/yì	ADV °rapidly ADJ easy VT change, exchange; despise; cultivate N the *Book of Changes*
耨	nòu	VT & VI °weed N hoe
壯	chuàng/zhuàng	ADJ strong, °able-bodied
暇	hsiá/xiá	ADJ & N leisure
日	jìh/rì	N °day, sun ADV daily
修	hsiū/xiū	VT °cultivate, arrange, reform; adorn, repair ADJ long, tall
忠	chūng/zhōng	N °loyalty VI be loyal to ADJ faithful
信	hsìn/xìn	N °good faith, trust ADJ trustworthy ADV truly VT trust
事	shìh/shì	VT °serve N service; affair
父	fù	N father
兄	hsiūng/xiōng	N elder brother

制	chìh/zhì	VT °prepare, make; regulate, control N regulation
梃	t'ǐng/tǐng	N stick
撻	t'à/tà	VT beat
堅	chiēn/jiān	ADJ firm, °strong, hard
彼	pǐ/bǐ	DEM PRON °they, that one, those DEM ADJ that, those
得	té/dé	VT get, obtain ADJ satisfied, complacent; fit, proper N success VI be finished; be ready V AUX may, °be able to
母	mǔ	N mother
凍	tùng/dòng	ADJ °cold VT freeze
弟	tì/dì	N younger brother
離	lí	ADJ °dispersed VT leave, depart from
散	sǎn	ADJ °scattered; undisciplined
	sàn	VT scatter, disperse, dismiss
陷	hsièn/xiàn	VT °entrap, defeat; fall into, sink in VI sink
溺	nì	VT °cause to sink VI sink, drown
往	wǎng	VI go out, set out, go to, °go N the past ADV formerly ADJ past, previous
誰	shuí	INT PRON who (also pronounced shéi)
敵	tí/dí	VT °be a match for, oppose N match, equal, enemy
故	kù/gù	CONJ °therefore, for this reason N cause, reason; the past ADJ old, former
疑	í/yí	VT °doubt ADJ doubtful

孟子 I.A.7

齊宣王[1]問曰："齊桓、晉文[2]之事可得聞乎？"

孟子對曰："仲尼[3]之徒無道[4]桓文之事者，是以[5]後世無傳焉[6]，臣未之聞也。無以[7]，則王乎？"

曰："德何如則可以王矣？"

曰："保民而王，莫之能禦也。"

曰："若寡人者，可以保民乎哉？"

曰："可。"

曰："何由[8]知吾可也？"

曰："臣聞之[9]胡齕曰，王坐於堂上，有牽牛而過堂下者，王見之，曰：'牛何之？'對曰：'將以釁鐘[10]。'王曰：'舍之！吾不忍其觳觫，若無罪而就死地。'對曰：'然則廢釁鐘與？'曰：'何可廢也？以羊易之！'— 不識有諸[11]？"

1　齊宣王: King Hsüan of Ch'i (r. 319-301 B.C.).

2　齊桓, Huan of Ch'i (r. 685-643 B.C.); 晉文, Wen of Chin (r. 636-627 B.C.). Two of the five overlords 霸 who held power during the Spring and Autumn period.

3　仲尼 Confucius' style or *tzù* 字; a style was a name taken on reaching maturity. His surname was K'ung 孔, and his given name was Ch'iu 丘.

4　道, to speak.

5　是以, because of this, therefore. Demonstrative pronouns sometimes stand before the preposition of which they are the object.

6　焉 fusion of 於之; the 之 refers to 後世.

7　以 here is interchangeable with 已, to stop.

8　何由, from what, how. An interrogative pronoun object stands before the preposition.

9　之 refers to the following anecdote told by Hu Ho 胡齕.

10　將以釁鐘 implies 將以之釁鐘. 之 is always omitted after 以.

11　At the end of a sentence 諸 is always a fusion of 之乎.

曰："有之。"

曰："是心足以王矣，百姓皆以王為¹愛也，臣固知王之不忍也。"

王曰："然²；誠有百姓³者。齊國雖褊小，吾何愛一牛？即不忍其觳觫，若無罪而就死地，故以羊易之也。"

曰："王無異於百姓之以王為愛也。以小易大，彼惡知之？王若⁴隱其無罪而就死地，則牛羊何擇焉？"

王笑曰："是誠何心哉？我非愛其財而易之以羊也。宜乎百姓之謂我愛也。"

曰："無傷也，是乃仁術也，見牛未見羊也。君子之於禽獸也，見其生，不忍見其死；聞其聲，不忍食其肉。是以君子遠庖廚也。"

王說曰："詩⁵云：'他人有心，予忖度之。'夫子之謂⁶也。夫我乃行之，反而求之，不得吾心。夫子言之，於我心有戚戚焉。此心之所以合於王者，何也？"

曰："有復於王者曰：'吾力足以舉百鈞，而不足以舉一羽；明足以察秋毫之末，而不見輿薪，則王許之乎？'"

---

1 以⋯為⋯, consider... to be....
2 然, yes, that is right.
3 百姓 in this context refers to the people who thought the king grudged the ox: such people.
4 若, if.
5 *Song* 198.
6 夫子之謂 here the pronoun object 之 resumes the topical subject 夫子 which is the grammatical object of 謂: master, [it] refers [to] you.

MENG-TZU I.A.7

曰："否。"

"今恩足以及禽獸，而功不至於百姓者，獨[1]何與？然則一羽之不舉，為不用力焉；輿薪之不見，為不用明焉；百姓之不見[2]保，為不用恩焉。故王之不王，不為也，非不能也。"

曰："不為者與不能者[3]之形何以異？"

曰："挾太山以超北海，語人曰，'我不能。'是誠不能也。為長者折枝，語人曰，'我不能。'是不為也，非不能也。故王之不王，非挾太山以超北海之類也；王之不王，是折枝之類也。

"老吾老[4]，以及[5]人之老；幼吾幼，以及人之幼。天下可運於掌。詩[6]云：'刑于寡妻，至于兄弟，以御于家邦。'言舉斯心加諸彼而已。故推恩足以保四海，不推恩無以保妻子。古之人所以大過人者，無他焉，善[7]推其所為而已矣。今恩足以及禽獸，而功不至於百姓者，獨何與？

"權，然後知輕重；度，然後知長短。物皆然，心為甚。王請度之！"

---

1 獨 strengthens the interrogative in rhetorical questions.
2 In front of a verb 見 makes the verb passive.
3 不為者與不能者 two nominal clauses joined by 與 and both qualifiying 形.
4 老吾老 the first 老 is a verb: treat the old people of your own family as they ought to be treated; the second is a noun: old people.
5 以及: 以(之)及.
6 *Song* 240.
7 In front of a verb 善 often means "be good at".

Vocabulary

宣	hsüān/xuān	N °a proper name VT spread, dissipate; proclaim; drain away
桓	huán	N °a proper name; pillar ADJ martial
文	wén	N °a proper name; markings, ornament; culture, writing, literature, a written composition ADJ elegant, cultured, civil
聞	wén	VI °be heard of VT hear N fame, reputation ADJ famous
仲	chùng/zhòng	N second (e.g., in order of birth)
尼	ní	N mountain; nun
	nǐ	VT stop
徒	t'ú/tú	N °follower, disciple; people of the same class VI go on foot ADV only, merely
世	shìh/shì	N °a generation, era; age, world ADJ hereditary
傳	ch'uán/chuán	VT °transmit, hand down
	chuàn/zhuàn	N record, biography, chronicle
臣	ch'én/chén	N subject, vassal, minister; °used by an official to refer to himself when addressing the king
德	té/dé	N °virtue, innate power; kindness, favour
保	pǎo/bǎo	VT °protect, guard, guarantee
能	néng	V AUX °be able to N ability
禦	yǜ/yù	VT °withstand, resist
哉	tsāi/zāi	PART final exclamatory particle
胡	hú	N °a proper name; tribes living to the north and west of China INT PRON what INT ADV why, how
齕	hó/hé	N °a proper name VI gnaw, nibble
坐	tsò/zuò	VI °sit VT try a case, find guilty, convict N seat
堂	t'áng/táng	N hall

牽	ch'iēn/qiān	VT °lead, pull, drag; implicate, connect
牛	niú	N ox, cow
過	kuò/guò	VT °pass, visit VI exceed N fault
釁	hsìn/xìn	VT °consecrate, smear with sacrificial blood N rift, wrong
鐘	chūng/zhōng	N bell
舍	shě	VT give up, °release; give alms
	shè	N lodging, house, shed VI stop for night
忍	jěn/rěn	VT °bear, be insensitive of (suffering in others) ADJ tolerant, insensitive
觳	hú	N ancient measure of capacity, goblet
觳觫	hú-sù	N °terror, frightened appearance
就	chiù/jiù	VT approach, °go to; accomplish
廢	fèi	VT °abandon, set aside, remove; destroy VI be discarded
羊	yáng	N sheep, goat
識	shíh/shí	VT °know, recognize
	chìh/zhì	VT record, remember (used for 誌) N mark; record (used for 誌)
諸	chū/zhū	PART fusion of PRON OBJ 之 + PREP 於; or °PRON OBJ 之 + INT PART 乎 ADJ various, all
足以	tsú-ǐ/zúyǐ	V AUX °sufficient to, adequate to, able to
姓	hsìng/xìng	N family name, surname
百姓	păi-hsìng/băixìng	N the people
皆	chiēh/jiē	ADV °all, in all cases, equally
愛	ài	VI °be grudging VT grudge, love, care for
固	kù/gù	ADV °truly, surely, firmly, certainly; originally; no doubt ADJ secure, firm VT solidify, stabilize
誠	ch'éng/chéng	ADV °truly, really ADJ sincere, honest N honesty, integrity

雖	suī	SUB CONJ °although, even if; even so
		ADJ even
褊	piěn/biǎn	ADJ tight, °narrow
小	hsiǎo/xiǎo	ADJ °small, little, mean, petty
		VT make or consider small, despise
即	chí/jí	ADV °(is) in fact, (is) precisely; at the time, at once
		SUB CONJ even if; then, accordingly
		VT go to, arrive
		PREP upon, at
惡	wù	VT detest, hate
	ò/è	ADJ ugly, hateful, evil
	wū	INT PRON what, where
		INT ADV °how, why
隱	yǐn	VT °feel pained or grieved by; conceal
		VI be hidden
		ADJ painful, concealed
	yìn	VT lean on
擇	tsé/zé	VT °choose, select; distinguish
財	ts'ái/cái	N °expense, wealth, valuables, resources
宜	í/yí	ADJ °right, proper
		ADV rightly
		VT cause to be fitting
		V AUX ought
謂	wèi	VT °describe, refer to (as), say to, tell
傷	shāng	N °harm, injury
		VT injure, hurt
乃	nǎi	ADV °(is) in fact
		SUB CONJ then; but
		PRON you
術	shù	N °artifice, art; method, skill
禽	ch'ín/qín	N a general word for birds
獸	shòu	N °a general word for beasts, wild beasts
聲	shēng	N °sound, voice
		VT sound
庖	p'áo/páo	N °kitchen; cook
廚	ch'ú/chú	N kitchen
說	yüèh/yuè	VI °be pleased (also written 悅)
	shuō	VT explain, advise
		N saying, explanation, theory

	shuì	VT persuade
詩	shīh/shī	N °*The Book of Songs*; poem, poetry
云	yǘn/yún	VT °say (used to indicate quotation); have; be
予	yǘ/yú	PRON °I
	yǚ/yǔ	VT give
忖	ts'ǔn/cǔn	VT consider
度	tó/duó	VT °consider, calculate, measure
	tù/dù	N measure, law
行	hsíng/xíng	VT °put into practice VI walk, travel; act N action, conduct
	háng	N road; row, line
言	yén/yán	VT °speak about VI speak N words
戚	ch'ī/qī	N pity; relative
戚戚	ch'ī-ch'ī/qīqī	N °feeling of sympathy, closeness or pity VT be touched, be moved
合	hó/hé	VI come together, °be compatible with, suit; enclose VT join, unite ADJ whole
復	fù	VI °report; reply; return VT report to; restore, repay; repeat ADV again N duplicate
力	lì	N °strength, force
舉	chǚ/jǔ	VT °raise, lift up; start; present ADV all
鈞	chūn/jūn	N °30 catties ADJ equal (used for 均) VT make equal (used for 均)
羽	yǚ/yǔ	N feather
明	míng	N °sight, understanding ADJ bright, clear; clear-sighted VT make bright; make clear, understand
秋	ch'iū/qiū	N °autumn; harvest time; year, a period of time
毫	háo	N °fine hair, down (on plants and birds) ADJ fine, minute

末	mò	N °tip of something, end of a brush ADJ secondary
輿	yű/yú	N °cart, carriage; the public; territory VT contain; hold
薪	hsīn/xīn	N firewood
許	hsǔ/xǔ	VT °agree, allow, permit, promise NUM unspecified number: about, or so, or more
否	fǒu	NEG ADV °no; it is not so; or not
恩	ēn	N kindness, grace, favour
功	kūng/gōng	N °merit, achievement, good results
獨	tú/dú	ADV °alone ADJ alone, solitary
形	hsíng/xíng	N °form, shape
挾	hsiéh/xié	VT °take under one's arm; use force, coerce
太	t'ài/tài	N °name of mountain (also written 泰) ADJ great
超	ch'āo/chāo	VT °leap over, excel
北	pěi/běi	N & ADJ °north VI be defeated
海	hǎi	N sea
語	yǔ/yǔ	VT °say to, tell N speech, talk, saying VI talk, speak
折	ché/zhé	VT °break, break off, bend; humble
枝	chīh/zhī	N branch of tree
類	lèi	N °category, sort, kind VI be of the same sort VT resemble
老	lǎo	VT °treat as the old ought to be treated ADJ old
幼	yù/yòu	VT °treat as the young ought to be treated ADJ young
運	yǜn/yùn	VI °revolve; move VT transport N destiny, fate
掌	chǎng/zhǎng	N °palm of hand VT manage
于	yű/yú	PREP same as 於

MENG-TZU I.A.7

御	yù/yù	VT °control, govern; drive a chariot N charioteer VI wait (on); present (to) ADJ imperial
邦	pāng/bāng	N state, country
推	t'uī/tuī	VT °extend, enlarge, push; push to logical conclusion; investigate; promote
古	kǔ/gǔ	N °the past, ancient times ADJ ancient
善	shàn	ADJ good, skilful
權	ch'üán/quán	VT °weigh N weight; power, authority
輕	ch'īng/qīng	ADJ °light; unimportant VT consider unimportant, look down upon
重	chùng/zhòng	ADJ °heavy; important VT consider important, respect
	ch'úng/chóng	VT double, repeat
短	tuǎn/duǎn	ADJ °short; deficient N shortcoming
物	wù	N thing, object
甚	shèn	N extreme ADJ °greater, more, excessive ADV very

孟子 I.B.2

齊宣王問曰："文王[1]之囿方七十里[2]，有諸？"

孟子對曰："於傳有之。"

曰："若是其大乎？"

曰："民猶以為小[3]也。"

曰："寡人之囿方四十里，民猶以為大，何也？"

曰："文王之囿方七十里，芻蕘者[4]往焉，雉兔者[5]往焉，與民同之。民以為小，不亦宜乎？臣始至於境，問國之大禁，然後[6]敢入。臣聞郊關之內有囿方四十里，殺其麋鹿者如殺人之罪。則是方四十里為阱於國中。民以為大，不亦宜乎？"

1　King Wen of Chou 周 was the father of King Wu 武, the founder of the Chou dynasty (11th century B.C.).
2　When numerals are used as predicates, they behave like adjectives, i.e., no copula verb is necessary.
3　以為小 implies 以之為小.
4　芻蕘者, one who gathers hay and stalks for fuel.
5　雉兔者, one who hunts for pheasants and hares.
6　然後 is a conjunction meaning "afterwards"; implies that the action of the verb in this clause can occur only after the completion of the action of the verb in the previous clause.

Vocabulary

囿	yù/yòu	N °park, garden VI limit
猶	yú/yóu	ADV °still VT equal (something), resemble VI be equal SUB CONJ still, yet
芻	ch'ú/chú	VT cut grass N °hay, straw
蕘	jáo/ráo	N fuel-gatherer; °stalks for fuel
雉	chìh/zhì	N pheasant
兔	t'ù/tù	N hare
同	t'úng/tóng	VT °share, join VI be the same ADV together
境	chìng/jìng	N °boundary, border; territory; situation
禁	chìn/jìn	N °prohibition VT prohibit, forbid
敢	kǎn/gǎn	V AUX °dare to, venture, presume
郊	chiāo/jiāo	N outskirts (of city)
關	kuān/guān	N °frontier pass or gate; door-bar VT shut, close
麋	mí	N deer
鹿	lù	N deer
阱	chǐng/jǐng	N trap (for animals)

孟子 I.B.6

孟子謂齊宣王曰："王之臣有託其妻子於其友而之楚遊者，比其反也，則凍餒其妻子，則如之何？"

王曰："棄之。"

曰："士師[1]不能治士，則如之何？"

王曰："已之。"

曰："四境之內不治，則如之何？"

王顧左右而言他。

---

1 士師, Chief Judge. Third-ranking executive post in the Ministry of Justice.

Vocabulary

託	t'ō/tuō	VT °entrust; plead, make excuses
友	yŭ/yǒu	N friend
遊	yú/yóu	VI rove around, °wander, travel, tour, roam; associate with
餒	něi	N hunger ADJ °hungry, putrid
師	shīh/shī	N teacher, °master; troops, army VI be an example VT treat as a teacher, imitate
治	chìh/zhì	VT °regulate, arrange, cultivate, govern ADJ well-governed
左	tsŏ/zuŏ	N left
右	yù/yòu	N right
左右	tsŏ-yù/zuǒyòu	N those to the left and right, i.e., attendants

孟子 I.B.7

孟子見齊宣王，曰："所謂故國者，非謂有喬木之謂也，有世臣之謂也。王無親臣矣，昔者所進，今日不知其亡也。"

王曰："吾何以識其不才而舍之？"

曰："國君進賢，如不得已[1]，將使卑踰尊，疏踰戚，可不慎與？左右皆曰賢，未可也；諸大夫皆曰賢，未可也；國人皆曰賢，然後察之；見賢焉，然後用之。左右皆曰不可，勿聽；諸大夫皆曰不可，勿聽；國人皆曰不可，然後察之；見不可焉，然後去之。左右皆曰可殺，勿聽；諸大夫皆曰可殺，勿聽；國人皆曰可殺，然後察之；見可殺焉，然後殺之。故曰，國人殺之也。如此，然後可以為民父母[2]。"

---

1 不得已, no alternative, the only thing possible.
2 In Confucian thought the ruler is often described as a parent to the people.

Vocabulary

喬	ch'iáo/qiáo	ADJ °tall, high, stately
昔	hsī/xī	ADV formerly
進	chìn/jìn	VT bring forward, °promote VI go up to, go forward, advance
亡	wáng	VI die, perish; °escape VT lose
	wú	VT not to have, not exist (interchangeable with 無)
才	ts'ái/cái	VI °be talented N talent, ability ADV just, only
賢	hsién/xián	N °the wise ADJ wise, worthy
卑	pēi/bēi	N °the humble ADJ low, humble
踰	yú/yú	VT °pass over, go beyond, exceed, surpass, cross
尊	tsūn/zūn	N °the honourable, noble; goblet VT honour
疏	shū	N °the distant ADJ wide apart, scattered, far off; coarse; careless VT dredge; divide
慎	shèn	VI be cautious
聽	t'īng/tīng	VT obey, °listen to; permit, allow
去	ch'ǜ/qù	VT °dismiss; leave, reject VI go away

孟子 I.B.15

滕文公1問曰:"滕,小國也;竭力以事大國,則2不得免焉,如之何則可?"

孟子對曰:"昔者大王3居邠,狄人侵之。事之以皮幣,不得免焉;事之以犬馬,不得免焉;事之以珠玉,不得免焉。乃4屬其耆老而告之曰:'狄人之所欲者,吾土地也。吾聞之也:君子不以其所以養人者害人。二三子5何患乎無君?我將去之。'去邠,踰梁山,邑于岐山之下居焉。邠人曰:'仁人也,不可失也。'從之者如歸市6。

"或曰:'世守7也,非身之所能為也。效死8勿去。'

"君請擇於斯二者。"

---

1 滕 was a small state to the south of Ch'i; it was situated between the two powerful states, Ch'i and Ch'u. Mencius visited it around 323-320 B.C.
2 則 here is used in a concessive meaning: yet, still.
3 大王, King T'ai, the posthumous title of Ku-kung Tan-fu 古公亶父, the grandfather of the founder of the 周 dynasty, King Wu 武王.
4 乃 is a conjunction: then, thereupon.
5 二三子, my disciples, my friends.
6 歸市, to go to the market, means "many, numerous".
7 世守 implies 世所守.
8 效死, be devoted to the point of death.

MENG-TZU I.B.15

Vocabulary

滕	t'éng/téng	N name of a small Chinese state
公	kūng/gōng	N duke; one of the ranks of nobility
竭	chiéh/jié	VT use to the full, exhaust
免	miěn/miǎn	VI °escape, avoid VT relieve
居	chū/jū	VT °live in VI dwell, settle down, occupy a place, sit
邠	pīn/bīn	N name of a state
狄	tí/dí	N °northern barbarians
	t'ì/tì	VT drive away, remove (used for 逖)
侵	ch'īn/qīn	VT invade, encroach upon, raid
皮	p'í/pí	N fur, skins
幣	pì/bì	N °length of silk; wealth, coin
犬	ch'üǎn/quǎn	N dog
馬	mǎ	N horse
珠	chū/zhū	N pearl
玉	yù/yù	N °jade ADJ jade-like, pure white
屬	chǔ/zhǔ	VT °assemble; be connected with; entrust to; enjoin
	shǔ	VT belong to, be attached to VI be attached, be dependent
耆	ch'í/qí	ADJ old
耆老	ch'í-lǎo/qílǎo	N elders
欲	yù/yù	VT °desire, long for, want V AUX wish to, intend ADV about to, on the point of
土	t'ǔ/tǔ	N °land, earth, dirt
害	hài	VT °harm, injure N injury
患	huàn	VI °be worried VT treat as a calamity N calamity
邑	ì/yì	VI °establish a city N city
岐	ch'í/qí	N °name of a mountain; mountain path ADJ precipitous

市	shìh/shì	N °market place VT sell, trade, buy
守	shǒu	VT °keep, guard, hold on to, preserve
效	hsiào/xiào	VT °devote, hand over, offer; imitate, follow; verify, fulfil N effect

孟子 VI.A.2

告子1曰："性猶湍水也，決諸2東方則東流，決諸西方則西流。人性之無分於善不善也，猶水之無分於東西也。"

孟子曰："水信無分於東西，無分於上下乎？人性之善也，猶水之就下也。人無有不善，水無有不下。今夫水，搏而躍之，可使過顙；激而行之，可使在山。是豈3水之性哉？其勢則然也。人之可使為不善，其性亦猶是也。"

---

1 告子: little is known about Kao-tzu. In the *Meng-tzu* a number of discussions between him and Mencius about human nature are recorded. Kao-tzu thought human nature was neutral, Mencius thought it was good.

2 諸 = 之於.

3 豈 indicates a rhetorical question, "how can it be", implying that it cannot be. When the verb is positive 豈 may be translated "surely it is not" and when it is negative "surely it is".

Vocabulary

性	hsìng/xìng	N °nature, disposition, inherent quality, temperament
湍	t'uān/tuān	ADJ °rushing (of water) N torrent
水	shuǐ	N water
決	chüéh/jué	VT °open up or clear (waterway), break (banks); decide; cut off V AUX decide to ADV decidedly, quickly
流	liú	VI °flow, drift VT circulate N flow, current ADJ drifting
分	fēn	VI °distinguish VT divide, share, distinguish, separate, apportion
	fèn	N part, share, allotment, division
搏	pó/bó	VT °strike, attack with hands, beat
躍	yüèh/yuè	VI skip, jump VT °cause to jump
顙	sǎng	N forehead
激	chī/jī	VI & VT °dam; arouse ADJ turbulent, violent
在	tsài/zài	VT be at, be in, °be on; consist in, depend on VI be alive, be present
豈	ch'ǐ/qǐ	INT ADV how, surely not
勢	shìh/shì	N °circumstances, conditions; force, power, strategic position

孟子 VI.A.10

孟子曰："魚，我所欲也，熊掌亦我所欲也；二者不可得兼，舍魚而取熊掌者也。生亦[1]我所欲也，義亦我所欲也；二者不可得兼，舍生而取義者也。生亦我所欲，所欲有甚於生者，故不為苟得也；死亦我所惡，所惡有甚於死者，故患有所不辟也。如使人之所欲莫甚於生，則凡可以得生者，何不用也？使人之所惡莫甚於死者，則凡可以辟患者，何不為也？由是則生而有不用也，由是則可以辟患而有不為也，是故所欲有甚於生者，所惡有甚於死者。非獨賢者有是心也，人皆有之，賢者能勿喪耳。一簞食、一豆羹，得之則生，弗[2]得則死，呼爾而與之，行道之人弗受[3]；蹴爾而與之，乞人不屑也；萬鍾[4]則不辯禮義而受之。萬鍾於我何加焉？為宮室之美、妻妾之奉、所識窮乏者得[5]我與？鄉為身死而不受，今為宮室之美為之；鄉為身死而不受，今為妻妾之奉為之；鄉為身死而不受，今為所識窮乏者得我而為之，是亦不可以已乎？此之謂失其本心。"

---

1 亦… 亦… conjunction: both…and…, and also.
2 弗 is used with transitive verbs as a fusion of 不之 which is not used.
3 This refers to an anecdote in the *Li-chi*; during a famine a man refused food offered to him in an impolite manner. He subsequently died.
4 萬鍾 refers to a high salary.
5 得 is here used for 德 and means "be grateful to".

Vocabulary

熊	hsiúng/xióng	N bear
兼	chiēn/jiān	ADV simultaneously, concurrently, equally. Original meaning: to hold two standing stalks of grain in one hand VT °have at the same time, unite in one VI double ADJ double, twice
辟	p'ì/pì	VT °avoid (also written 避); open up (territory), develop (also written 闢) N depravity ADJ depraved
凡	fán	ADJ commonplace, ordinary; every, °in all cases, all ADV in all; generally, in general
簞	tān/dān	N °bamboo dish, basket
豆	tòu/dòu	N legumes, pulses, beans; °stemmed cup or bowl
羹	kēng/gēng	N thick soup
弗	fú	NEG ADV a negative similar to 不
呼	hū	VT call, shout; address; commend; breathe out
	hù	VT °insult, berate
爾	ěrh/ěr	PART a final particle: like this, and that is all ADV SUF °-like, -ly PRON you DEM PRON this, that
受	shòu	VT receive, accept; be subjected to; suffer, bear
蹴	ts'ù/cù	VT °trample, kick VI step on; kick
屑	hsièh/xiè	N bits, crumbs, scraps ADJ trifling VT break into pieces, smash; °consider worthwhile, pay attention to
鍾	chūng/zhōng	N round shaped pot; °measure for grain approx. 64 斗 tǒu/dǒu or 6.4 litres VT concentrate, gather
辯	pièn/biàn	VI & VT debate, argue; °differentiate, distinguish (also written 辨); administer; change (also written 變)
禮	lǐ	N °rite, ritual, propriety, ceremony
宮	kūng/gōng	N °palace, dwelling, temple

MENG-TZU VI.A.10

美	měi	ADJ beautiful, handsome, pretty; good, satisfactory, admirable N good thing, °the beautiful, beauty, elegance VT praise
奉	fèng	VT offer with both hands; receive respectfully; °wait on, serve
窮	ch'iúng/qióng	ADJ exhausted; °poor, reduced to extremity; blocked; unsuccessful VT exhaust, investigate thoroughly
乏	fá	VI & VT lack; delay ADJ incapable, useless, tired, °poor
鄉	hsiāng/xiāng	N the country, village, district; hometown
	hsiàng/xiàng	N direction; tendency (used for 向) ADV °previously, before, in the past, formerly (used for 向)
本	pěn/běn	N basis, origin, root, tree trunk ADJ °original ADV really, originally

孟子 II.A.6

孟子曰："人皆有不忍人之心。先王[1]有不忍人之心，斯有不忍人之政矣。以不忍人之心，行不忍人之政，治天下可運之掌上。所以謂人皆有不忍人之心者，今人乍見孺子將入於井，皆有怵惕惻隱之心 — 非所以內交[2]於孺子之父母也，非所以要譽於鄉黨朋友也，非惡其聲而然也。由是觀之，無惻隱之心，非人也；無羞惡之心，非人也；無辭讓之心，非人也；無是非之心，非人也。惻隱之心，仁之端也；羞惡之心，義之端也；辭讓之心，禮之端也；是非之心，智之端也。人之有是四端也，猶其有四體也。有是四端而自[3]謂不能者，自賊者也；謂其君不能者，賊其君者也。凡有四端於我者，知皆擴而充之矣，若火之始然[4]，泉之始達。苟能充之，足以保四海；苟不充之，不足以事父母。"

---

1 先王 refers to the sage kings of antiquity.
2 內交, to be acquainted with, to be associated with.
3 自 always stands in front of the verb. Before VT it indicates that the subject and the object are the same; before VI or VT + OBJ it stresses that it is the subject that is acting.
4 然, usually written 燃, to burn.

Vocabulary

乍	chà/zhà	ADV °suddenly, unexpectedly; just
孺	jú/rú	N °child, baby
井	chǐng/jǐng	N well
怵	ch'ù/chù	VI be frightened
惕	t'ì/tì	VI °be alarmed ADJ timorous
惻	ts'è/cè	VI °be distressed VT pity
要	yāo	VT °seek, demand
	yào	ADJ important, essential
譽	yǜ/yù	VT praise N °praise; fame, reputation
黨	tǎng/dǎng	N °village, clique, faction; kinsfolk, relatives VI be partial to; take sides with
朋	p'éng/péng	N °friend, equal
辭	tz'ú/cí	VT °decline, refuse; take leave of N word, phrase
讓	jàng/ràng	VT yield, cede
端	tuān/duān	N °beginning, tip, end; clue; reason ADJ upright, straight VI start, begin
智	chìh/zhì	ADJ intelligent, wise N °wisdom
體	t'ǐ/tǐ	N body; substance; °limbs; style, form VT rely on
自	tzù/zì	ADV °self PREP from
賊	tsé/zé	VT °injure, plunder (also pronounced *tséi/zéi*) N bandit, thief (also pronounced *tséi/zéi*)
擴	k'uò/kuò	VT expand, stretch, enlarge
充	ch'ūng/chōng	VT °extend, enlarge; fill, satisfy ADJ full
火	huǒ	N °fire VT set fire to
泉	ch'üán/quán	N °spring, source

Han Fei-tzu 韓非子

HAN Fei (c.280-c.233 B.C.) belonged to the royal family of Han. For a time he studied with the Confucian scholar, Hsün-tzu. Han Fei, whose aim was to create a rich and strong state ruled by an absolute monarch, disapproved of the way in which the king of Han was ruling the state; his remonstrances, however, had no effect. In 234 B.C., Ch'in prepared to attack the state of Han. In the hope of saving the state the king sent Han Fei to Ch'in where he was welcomed with delight. However, a former fellow student, Li Ssu 李斯, brought accusations against Han Fei which led to his death.

The *Han-fei-tzu* brings together various strands of thought—law (*fa* 法), methods of government (*shu* 術) and authority (*shih* 勢)—which form the basis of the political philosophy of the Legalists 法家. The style is logical, well structured and well argued and the grammar is consistent. The *Han-fei-tzu* had an important influence on later writing and political thought.

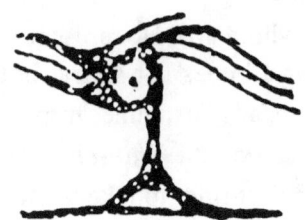

韓非子 和氏 c.13

楚人和氏¹得玉璞楚山中²,奉而獻之厲王³,厲王使玉人相⁴之,玉人曰:"石也。"王以和為誑,而刖其左足。及厲王薨,武王⁵即位,和又奉其璞而獻之武王,武王使玉人相之,又曰:"石也。"王又以和為誑,而刖其右足。武王薨,文王⁶即位,和乃抱其璞而哭於楚山之下,三日三夜,泣盡而繼之以血。王聞之,使人問其故,曰:"天下之刖者多矣,子奚哭之悲也?"和曰:"吾非悲刖也,悲夫寶玉而題之以石,貞士而名之以誑,此吾所以悲也。"王乃使玉人理其璞而得寶焉。遂命曰:"和氏之璧。"

---

1 His name is sometimes given as 卞和 Pien Ho.
2 Implies 得玉璞於楚山中.
3 The list of kings to whom Mr Ho presented the jade varies in different versions of this story. King Li does not appear in the traditional chronology.
4 相 here is a verb and means "examine, inspect".
5 Dates for King Wu, based on the *Shih-chi* 史記, are 740-690 B.C. According to the *Shih-chi*, he was the first ruler to take the title of 王 in Ch'u.
6 Dates for King Wen, based on the *Shih-chi*, are 689-677 B.C.

Vocabulary

韓	hán	N °a proper name, name of a small Chinese state
和	hó/hé	N °a surname; harmony, peace ADJ mild, harmonious VT mix, blend
	hò/hè	VT harmonize with, make harmonious
氏	shìh/shì	N clan, family, surname, °a title: Mr, Miss
璞	p'ú/pú	N unpolished jade
獻	hsièn/xiàn	VT present, offer respectfully
厲	lì	N °a proper name; whetstone VT grind, discipline ADJ stern, severe
石	shíh/shí	N °stone, rock
	tàn/dàn	N a measure for grain
誑	k'uáng/kuáng	VT & VI °deceive, exaggerate
刖	yüèh/yuè	VT cut off feet (as punishment)
薨	hūng/hōng	N death of a ruler VI °die
武	wǔ	N °a name ADJ martial
位	wèi	N position, rank; seat, °throne; location VI be located
即位	chí-wèi/jíwèi	VI ascend the throne
抱	pào/bào	VT °carry in arms, embrace, cherish, enfold, grasp
哭	k'ū/kū	VI weep
夜	yèh/yè	N °night, darkness
繼	chì/jì	VT °continue, follow after
血	hsüèh/xuè	N blood
奚	hsī/xī	INT ADV °why, how INT PRON what, where
悲	pēi/bēi	VI feel sad VT feel sad about, grieve for ADJ grievous, sad N °sadness
寶	pǎo/bǎo	ADJ °precious, rare, valuable VT consider precious

HAN-FEI-TZU c. 13

題	t'í/tí	VT °label; bring to notice N forehead; heading, theme
貞	chēn/zhēn	ADJ °upright, sincere, loyal, pure VT divine
名	míng	N name, reputation, fame VT °name
理	lǐ	VT °cut and polish jade; regulate N pattern or principle of things
遂	suì	CONJ °accordingly, consequently, then, thereupon VT follow, satisfy, fulfil
命	mìng	N order; mandate; destiny VT °name, term; order
璧	pì/bì	N jade disk with a hole in the centre

韓非子 難一 c.36

楚人有鬻楯與矛者，譽之曰："吾楯之堅，莫能陷也。"又譽其矛曰："吾矛之利，於物[1]無不陷也。"或曰："以子之矛，陷子之楯，何如？"其人弗能應也。夫不可陷之楯與無不陷之矛，不可同世而立。

韓非子 外儲説左上 c.32

鄭人有且置[2]履者，先自度其足而置之其坐。至之市而忘操之。已得履，乃曰："吾忘持度。"反歸取之。及反，市罷，遂不得履。人曰："何不試之以足？"曰："寧信度，無自信也。"

---

1 於物: the preposition 於 shows relationship between the preceding clause and 物. The phrase may be translated "in regard to things".

2 置, here means "to buy"; the second time it occurs in this line it means "to put, place".

Vocabulary

難	nàn	N °criticism; difficulty, calamity, trouble
	nán	ADJ difficult, troublesome
鬻	yǔ/yù	VT sell
楯	tùn/dùn	N °shield, parapet
矛	máo	N °spear, lance
應	yìng	VI agree; deal with VT °reply, respond to N answer
	yīng	V AUX ought
儲	ch'ǔ/chǔ	VT collect, store
鄭	chèng/zhèng	N °name of one of the ancient Chinese states; a surname ADJ solemn
且	ch'iěh/qiě	CONJ and, also, but also, moreover ADV still, °about to, on the point of, almost, nearly
置	chìh/zhì	VT place; set up, establish; dismiss, put aside; °buy
履	lǔ	N °shoes; footstep VT put on shoes VI tread on, walk on; carry out
忘	wàng	VT forget
操	ts'āo/cāo	VT °bring, take; grasp, hold; handle, operate N exercise, behaviour
持	ch'íh/chí	VT °bring, take; hold, grasp; manage; support, maintain
罷	pà/bà	VI °end, finish; stop, cease, remove (from office)
	p'í/pí	ADJ weary
試	shìh/shì	VT °try, test, examine; use N test
寧	nìng	ADV °it is better, rather, would rather
	níng	ADJ peaceful

韓非子　五蠹　c.49

　上古之世，人民少而禽獸眾，人民不勝禽獸蟲蛇。有聖人作，構木為巢以避群害，而民悅之，使王天下，號之曰有巢氏。民食果蓏蚌蛤，腥臊惡臭而傷害腹胃，民多疾病。有聖人作，鑽燧取火，以化腥臊，而民悅之，使王天下，號之曰燧人氏。中古之世，天下大水，而鯀、禹[1]決瀆。近古之世，桀、紂[2]暴亂，而湯、武[3]征伐。今有構木鑽燧於夏后氏[4]之世者，必為鯀、禹笑矣；有決瀆於殷[5]、周之世者，必為湯、武笑矣。然則今有美堯、舜[6]、湯、武、禹之道於當今之世者，必為新聖笑矣。是以聖人不期修古，不法常可[7]，論世之事，因為之備。宋人有耕田者，田中有株，兔走觸株，折頸而死，因釋其耒而守株，冀復得兔；兔不可復得，而身為宋國笑。今欲以先王之政，治當世之民，皆守株之類也。

1　鯀, name of legendary figure, the father of Yü 禹 (see below); he plays a prominent part in the flood myth; he attempted to dam up the waters without success. 禹, name of a legendary ruler, the founder of the Hsia 夏 dynasty (trad. in 2205 B.C.). Before he became ruler, he was ordered to bring the flood under control; he dug channels to drain the waters into the sea and succeeded.
2　桀, the last ruler of the Hsia dynasty (c.21st-c.16th century B.C), reputedly a tyrant. 紂, the last ruler of the Shang 商 dynasty (c.16th-11th century B.C.), also reputedly a tyrant.
3　湯, founder of the Shang dynasty (trad. in 1766 B.C.). 武, founder of the Chou 周 dynasty (trad. in 1122 B.C.).
4　夏后氏 is 禹.
5　殷, name used for the Shang dynasty after the capital was moved to Yin.
6　堯 and 舜, names of legendary sage rulers.
7　常可, constant practices.

Vocabulary

蠹	tù/dù	N °borer; moth VT eat, bore through; destroy, damage
眾	chùng/zhòng	N the whole (of a large group), multitude ADJ °many, numerous
蟲	ch'úng/chóng	N insect
蛇	shé	N °snake, serpent
聖	shèng	ADJ °wise N sage
作	tsò/zuò	VI °appear, arise; act, function VT make, do, compose
搆	kòu/gòu	VT °put up, lay frame; construct, form, compose; fabricate, make up; implicate, provoke (also written 構)
巢	ch'áo/cháo	N nest
避	pì/bì	VT & VI °avoid, evade, shun; prevent, keep away
群	ch'ún/qún	ADJ °all, numerous VI flock, form group N flock, group, crowd
悅	yüèh/yuè	VI be pleased VT °be pleased with, take delight in
號	hào	N name, assumed name, studio name; order; mark, sign VT °declare, call
	háo	VT howl, yell N howl
果	kuǒ/guǒ	ADJ full, satisfied N °fruit; result ADJ resolute, determined
蓏	lǒ/luǒ	N °melon, gourd
蚌	pàng/bàng	N °freshwater mussel; clam
蛤	kó/gé	N °clam
	há	N frog
腥	hsīng/xīng	N raw meat or fish; rank smell ADJ °stinking, fishy
臊	sāo	N foul smell, rank smell, rancid ADJ °foul
	sào	ADJ shy, bashful
臭	ch'òu/chòu	N smell, odour ADJ °stinking

腹	fù	N belly, stomach
胃	wèi	N stomach
疾	chí/jí	VT criticize; dislike, envy N °illness, defect ADJ anxious, hurried
病	pìng/bìng	VI be ill; be distressed N °sickness, fault, defect
鑽	tsuān/zuān	VT penetrate, pierce, bore, °strike (flint)
	tsuàn/zuàn	N drill
燧	suì	N beacon fire; °flint
化	huà	VT °transform, change; convert, influence VI melt, dissolve; burn up; die
鯀	kǔn/gǔn	N a proper name
禹	yǔ/yǔ	N a proper name
瀆	tú/dú	N ditch, drain, channel VT profane; be rude to
近	chìn/jìn	ADJ near, recent
桀	chiéh/jié	N a proper name
紂	chòu/zhòu	N a proper name
暴	pào/bào	ADJ °cruel, violent, savage; abrupt ADV violently
	p'ù/pù	VT expose to sun; dry in the sun (also written 曝)
亂	luàn	VT confuse, bring disorder to VI °cause disorder N rebellion, disorder
湯	t'āng/tāng	N °a proper name; hot liquid, soup
伐	fá	VT cut down, °attack, chastise
夏	hsià/xià	N summer; a proper name; °the Hsia dynasty
后	hòu	N king, empress ADV used for 後
殷	yīn	N °the Yin dynasty; a proper name ADJ substantial, rich
周	chōu/zhōu	N °the Chou dynasty; a surname ADJ complete, entire, whole, comprehensive; everywhere VT assist; encircle
堯	yáo	N a proper name
舜	shùn	N °a proper name; hibiscus

當	tāng/dāng	VT °be at, on or in (a certain place or time); occupy, undertake; match, equal to, resist PREP at, on; in presence of
	tàng/dàng	ADJ matching, appropriate, right VT treat as, regard as
新	hsīn/xīn	ADJ new, °recent; fresh
期	chī/jī	N full period (of one year, one month or one day)
	ch'ī/qī	N time, occasion; rendezvous VI set a time, make an appointment VT & VI °expect, hope
法	fǎ	N law, model, method VT °treat as a model
常	ch'áng/cháng	ADJ ordinary, normal; °constant, fixed ADV constantly, often, frequently; ever, once (used for 嘗) N constant virtues such as benevolence, righteousness, propriety, wisdom and fidelity; constant human relationships
論	lùn	VT °evaluate; examine critically; discuss; argue N a prose genre
	lún	N order, sequence (used for 倫) VT critically examine authenticity. This pronunciation is used in 論語, the *Analects*.
因	yīn	CONJ °accordingly VT rely on, follow, accord with PREP according to, because of N cause
備	pèi/bèi	VT equip; °prepare, get ready; complete N equipment, back wall ADV fully; in every possible way
宋	sùng/sòng	N a proper name, °name of one of the ancient Chinese states
株	chū/zhū	N °trunk of tree, stem of plant, individual plant, plant; tree root above ground
觸	ch'ù/chù	VT touch, contact; °hit, strike; emotionally affect another person
頸	chǐng/jǐng	N neck
釋	shìh/shì	VT explain; clear up; discard, °set aside, put away, let go, release; be relieved of ADJ Buddhist
耒	lěi	N a fork for digging
冀	chì/jì	VT hope

韓非子 二柄 c.7

　明主之所導制其臣者，二柄而已矣。二柄者，刑德也。何謂刑德？曰：殺戮之謂刑，慶賞之謂德。為人臣者[1]畏誅罰而利慶賞，故人主自用其刑德，則群臣畏其威而歸其利矣。故[2]世之姦臣則不然，所惡則能得之其主而罪之[3]，所愛則能得之其主而賞之。今人主非使賞罰之威利出於己也，聽其臣而行其賞罰，則一國之人皆畏其臣而易其君，歸其臣而去其君矣，此人主失刑德之患也。夫虎之所以能服狗者，爪牙也，使虎釋其爪牙而使狗用之，則虎反服於狗矣。人主者，以刑德制臣者也，今君人者，釋其刑德而使臣用之，則君反制於臣矣。

1　為人臣者, ministers.
2　故 here means "but". This is a rare usage.
3　The first 之 refers to punishment or the power to punish, the second to those the evil ministers hate.

Vocabulary

柄	pǐng/bǐng	N °handle, power
主	chǔ/zhǔ	N °ruler, lord, master VI be ruled VT rule over ADJ principal, chief
導	tǎo/dǎo	VT °guide, lead; instruct
戮	lù	N °execution VT kill in war, massacre; disgrace
慶	ch'ìng/qìng	N °reward; good luck VT reward; congratulate
賞	shǎng	N °reward VT reward, bestow, grant; enjoy
畏	wèi	VT be afraid of, stand in awe of
誅	chū/zhū	N °punishment (usually capital punishment) VT punish (usually by death), eradicate
威	wēi	N °prestige, majesty ADJ stern, majestic, awe-inspiring VT overawe
姦	chiēn/jiān	ADJ °wicked, treacherous; crafty, villainous N traitor
己	chǐ/jǐ	PRON oneself N the sixth of the ten heavenly stems
虎	hǔ	N tiger
服	fú	VT °subdue; wear VI submit N clothes, mourning garments
爪	chǎo/zhǎo	N °claws, talons VT claw, scratch
牙	yá	N teeth, °fangs

K'ung-tzu Chia-yü 孔子家語

THE *K'ung-tzu Chia-yü* (the school sayings of Confucius) is a collection of pre-Han and early Han accounts and anecdotes about Confucius as well as sayings attributed to him. The existing version was compiled by Wang Su 王肅 (195-256 A.D.). Wang said in his preface that a former student who was a descendant of Confucius brought him the manuscript of the work. Much of the material it contains can be found in other works, such as the *Tso-chuan*, and some of it was possibly later added by Wang Su.

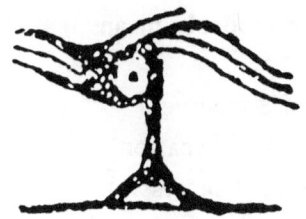

孔子家語 致思 c.8

孔子[1]適齊，中路，聞哭者之聲，其音甚哀。孔子謂其僕曰："此哭哀則哀矣，然非喪者之哀也。"驅而前，少進，見有異人焉。擁鎌帶索[2]，哭音不哀[3]。

孔子下車，追而問曰："子何人也。"

對曰："吾邱吾子也。"

曰："子今非喪之所[4]，奚哭之悲也。"

邱吾子曰："吾有三失，晚而自覺，悔之何及。"

曰："三失可得聞乎？願子告吾，無隱也。"

邱吾子曰："吾少時好學，周遍天下，後還，喪吾親，是一失也；長事齊君，君驕奢失士，臣節不遂[5]，是二失也；吾平生厚交，而今皆離絕，是三失也。夫樹欲靜而風不停，子欲養而親不待。往而不來者，年也；不可再見者，親也。請從此辭。"遂投水而死。

孔子曰："小子識之，斯足為戒矣。"自是弟子辭歸養親者十有[6]三。

---

1 孔子, Master K'ung is Confucius (551-479 B.C.).
2 擁鎌帶索: this expression probably means that the man held himself in low esteem.
3 哀 here means the grief of a mourner.
4 所 here means "circumstance, occasion".
5 不遂, did not succeed, was not successful.
6 有 = 又, and.

Vocabulary

孔	k'ǔng/kǒng	N °a surname; hole VT penetrate ADV very
致	chìh/zhì	VT send, convey to; extend to; °express; cause, result in; devote to N demeanour
思	ssū/sī	VI think, consider; think of N °thought
適	shìh/shì	VT suit; °go to, come to ADJ agreeable, suitable ADV just then, just now
音	yīn	N °sound, musical tone; pronunciation
哀	āi	ADJ °pitiful, sorrowful N grief, mourning
僕	p'ú/pú	N servant, °charioteer, footman
驅	ch'ū/qū	VI hasten gallop; °hurry VT drive forward; expel, disperse
前	ch'ién/qián	N front ADJ before, former ADV formerly VI °go or come forward
擁	yūng/yōng	VI be stopped, obstructed VT °hold; crowd, hem in ADJ knotty, knobbly
鐮	lién/lián	N °sickle
帶	tài/dài	VT take, bring, carry; °be girdled with; wear N belt, girdle; tape; district
索	sŏ/suŏ	N °rope VT search into; demand ADV alone
車	ch'ē/chē	N carriage, cart
追	chuī/zhuī	VT °overtake, pursue; trace out; seek for
邱	ch'iū/qiū	N a surname; mound (used for 丘)
晚	wǎn	N evening, night ADV °late ADJ late; younger (short for 晚生)
覺	chüéh/jué chiào/jiào	VT feel, perceive, °be conscious of VT wake from sleep
悔	huǐ	VT °regret N fault, blame

65

學	hsüéh/xué	N °study, learning VT study; imitate, copy
還	huán	VT go back, °come back; give back, return, do something in return
	hái	ADV still, yet; also, as well; even
奢	shē	ADJ luxurious, °extravagant
節	chiéh/jié	N joint or knot in bamboo; moral integrity; seasonal festival; tally; economy, restraint; virtue, purity VT abridge; °restrain; economize
平	p'íng/píng	ADJ flat, even; equal, fair; calm; °whole, all, average VT suppress, put in order, pacify, settle VI be pacified, be level, be equal
厚	hòu	ADJ thick, deep; kind, generous; °close VT favour; be generous to
絕	chüéh/jué	VT °cut off, sever; be exhausted; interrupt ADJ desperate; unique ADV absolutely
離絕	lí-chüéh/líjué	VI break off relations
靜	chìng/jìng	ADJ still, quiet
風	fēng	N °wind; ballad; custom; manner, style VT winnow VI teach, influence
	fèng	VT sway; persuade
停	t'íng/tíng	VI & VT °stop VT delay, stay
待	tài/dài	VT °wait for, wait upon; treat; entertain; need
年	nién/nián	N °year, harvest, age ADJ annual, yearly
再	tsài/zài	ADV another time, °again, once more; then, furthermore
投	t'óu/tóu	VT °throw into, throw; cast; put in, drop into; travel quickly towards; approach; give (present) VI fit in with; get on with
戒	chièh/jiè	VI guard against VT warn; give up; stop N °warning; Buddhist monastic discipline

Ta-hsüeh 大學

THE *Ta-hsüeh* (great learning) is a chapter of the *Li-chi* 禮記, the *Book of Rites*, a collection of ancient usages and rules of behaviour, of controversial date and origin. During the Sung dynasty, Chu Hsi 朱熹 (1130-1200) combined the *Ta-hsüeh*, the *Chung-yung* 中庸 (doctrine of the mean), the *Lun-yü* and the *Meng-tzu* into the *Four Books* which became the basis of classical education till the end of the imperial era.

The *Ta-hsüeh* is a concise statement of Confucian moral and political philosophy. The style is very simple; the passage is arranged in groups of parallel clauses which give it a rhythmical quality ideal for memorization.

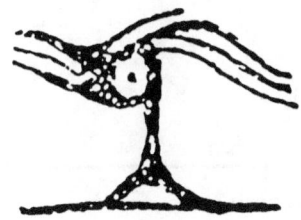

禮記 大學 c.42

大學之道在明明[1]德，在親民，在止於至善。知止而后[2]有定，定而后能靜，靜而后能安，安而后能慮，慮而后能得。物有本末，事有終始。知所先後則近道矣。古之欲明明德於天下者先治其國。欲治其國者先齊其家。欲齊其家者先修其身。欲修其身者先正其心。欲正其心者先誠其意。欲誠其意者先致其知。致知在格物。物格而后知至。知至而后意誠。意誠而后心正。心正而后身修。身修而后家齊。家齊而后國治。國治而后天下平。

---

1 The first 明 is a causative verb.
2 而后 = 而後.

Vocabulary

記	chì/jì	N note, notice; °record, written account; mark VT remember; record; mark
定	tìng/dìng	VI °be settled, fixed VT settle ADJ peaceful, settled
安	ān	ADV contentedly, peacefully, quietly ADJ contented, peaceful, quiet, safe VI be settled, °be secure INT ADV how INT PRON where, what
慮	lù	VI consider, think of, deliberate, plan, °think ahead; be anxious N anxiety
正	chèng/zhèng	VI be corrected VT °correct, make straight N straight, right ADV exactly, just
意	ì/yì	N meaning, idea; opinion; °intention; hint, suggestion VT anticipate, expect
格	kó/gé	VI arrive, come VT reach; °investigate, study exhaustively; correct N rule, pattern, style; trellis

Yen-tzu Ch'un-ch'iu 晏子春秋

THE *Yen-tzu Ch'un-ch'iu* is a collection of anecdotes about Yen Ying 晏嬰 (?-c.500 B.C.) who was a minister of Ch'i 齊 during the Spring and Autumn period. Many of the stories centre around remonstrances to Duke Ching 景 of Ch'i. Master Yen was renowned for his diplomatic skills and for his eloquence.

A book of this name was known in the Han dynasty; it was collated and edited by Liu Hsiang 劉向 (79-8 B.C.) who called it *Yen-tzu*. The text appears to come from the Chou dynasty, but there is disagreement on the actual date of composition. Some scholars believe that it was written by the disciples of Yen Ying some time before 400 B.C., while others ascribe it to the late Warring States period.

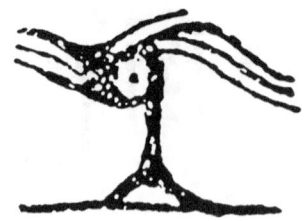

晏子春秋 c.6

晏子將使楚。楚王聞之，謂左右曰："晏嬰，齊之習辭[1]者也。今方來，吾欲辱之，何以也？"

左右對曰："為[2]其來也，臣請縛一人，過王而行。王曰：'何為者也？'對曰：'齊人也。'王曰：'何坐[3]。'曰：'坐盜。'"

晏子至，楚王賜晏子酒，酒酣，吏二縛一人詣王。王曰："縛者曷為者也。？"

對曰："齊人也，坐盜。"王視晏子曰："齊人固善盜乎？"

晏子避席[4]對曰："嬰聞之，橘生淮南則為橘，生於淮北則為枳，葉徒相似，其實味不同。所以然者何？水土異也。今民生長於齊不盜，入楚則盜，得無楚之水土使民善盜耶？"

王笑曰："聖人非所與熙也，寡人反取病焉。"

---

1 習辭, to be skilled in rhetoric; eloquent.
2 為, at that time, when. This is a rare usage.
3 坐, to commit a crime.
4 避席, to move away from someone's mat as a sign of respect. Mats were used to sit on.

Vocabulary

晏	yèn/yàn	N °a surname ADJ fine, sunny; bright-coloured; peaceful; late
春	ch'ūn/chūn	N spring
春秋	ch'ūn-ch'iū/ chūnqiū	N °chronological history; time, age; a period in ancient China
嬰	yīng	N °a proper name; infant VT tie something around the neck; bind; surround
習	hsí/xí	VT °be skilled/versed in; practise, review; study VI move wings rapidly; be accustomed to
縛	fù	VT bind something with a rope, °tie up; constrain
盜	tào/dào	VT steal, rob N °robbery; thief, robber; evil
賜	tz'ù/cì	VT °give, bestow (on inferior); grant
酣	hān	VT (drink etc.) to one's heart's content
吏	lì	N official, °soldier
詣	ì/yì	VT °go to, come to N (academic or technical) attainment
曷	hó/hé	INT PRON & INT ADJ °what INT ADV why, why not
視	shìh/shì	VT °look at, gaze at; regard
席	hsí/xí	N °mat; seat, place; feast, banquet
橘	chű/jú	N orange tree, tangerine tree
淮	huái	N name of a river
枳	chǐh/zhǐ	N trifoliate orange, a thorny orange tree bearing small fruit with thick skin
葉	yèh/yè	N °leaf, foliage; leaf-like thing; page; generation
似	ssù/sì	VT °resemble, be like ADV as though, seemingly
實	shíh/shí	N °fruit, seed; reality, fact, truth ADJ solid; true, real ADV really
味	wèi	N taste, flavour
耶	yéh/yé	PART final interrogative particle
熙	hsī/xī	ADJ bright, sunny; prosperous; gay VI °play, joke, sport

Lieh-tzu 列子

MASTER Lieh is Lieh Yü-k'ou 列禦寇 believed to have lived around 400 B.C. He is depicted in the *Chuang-tzu* as a mystic with spiritual powers. The book bearing his name is Taoist in inspiration and often uses fables and parables to elucidate its philosophy. Some of the stories also appear in other sources, such as the *Chuang-tzu* itself.

The earliest mention of this book is in a report written by Liu Hsiang in 14 B.C., the authenticity of which is doubted by some scholars. After that there is only one mention of this work until the fourth century A.D.

列子 湯問 c.5

伯牙善鼓琴，鍾子期[1]善聽。伯牙鼓琴，志在登高山。鍾子期曰："善哉！峨峨兮若泰山！"志在流水。鍾子期曰："善哉！洋洋兮若江河！"伯牙所念，鍾子期必得之。伯牙游於泰山之陰，坐[2]逢暴雨，止於巖下；心悲，乃援琴而鼓之。初為霖雨之操[3]，更造崩山之音。曲每奏，鍾子期輒窮其趣。伯牙乃舍琴而嘆曰："善哉！善哉！子之聽夫！志想象猶吾心也。吾於何逃聲哉！"

---

1 伯牙 Po-ya and 鍾子期 Chung Tzu-ch'i: Po-ya was an expert zither player. He became friends with a woodcutter called Chung Tzu-ch'i who was the only person able to fully appreciate Po-ya's musical skill. When Chung died, Po-ya smashed his zither and never played again.
2 坐, abruptly, unexpectedly, suddenly.
3 操, a tune.

Vocabulary

列	lièh/liè	N °a surname, row, rank, list VT arrange, rank, line up ADJ various
伯	pó/bó	N °a surname, father's elder brother; senior, a rank of nobility NUM one hundred (used for 百)
琴	ch'ín/qín	N °a seven-stringed instrument similar to a zither, often translated "lute"; a general name for stringed instruments
志	chìh/zhì	N °aim, idea, purpose, will, ideal
登	tēng/dēng	VT °ascend, mount; step on, tread
高	kāo/gāo	ADJ °high, tall, lofty; noble VI excel
峨	ó/é	ADJ high, lofty
兮	hsī/xī	PART used after adjectives to emphasize circumstances; exclamatory particle
泰	t'ài/tài	N °name of mountain ADJ extreme, exalted; excessive VI be extravagant
洋	yáng	ADJ °vast, extensive N ocean
江	chiāng/jiāng	N °large river; the Yangtze River
念	nièn/niàn	VT °think of, miss, consider; read aloud N thought, idea
游	yú/yóu	VI swim, float; travel about; °roam (used for 遊)
陰	yīn	N the feminine or negative principle in nature; °the shady side, i.e., the north side of a hill or the south side of a river; the nether world; back; moon
逢	féng	VT °meet; come upon
雨	yǔ/yǔ	N rain
巖	yén/yán	N rock, °cliff ADJ precipitous
援	yüán/yuán	VT pull by hand, lead, °hold; quote; help, rescue
初	ch'ū/chū	N the beginning, the first ADV °at first, in the beginning ADJ elementary, original
霖	lín	N continuous heavy rain

LIEH-TZU c. 5

更	kēng/gēng	VT change, replace; alternate; experience N one of the five two-hour watches into which the night was divided
	kèng/gèng	ADV more, even more; again; °further
造	tsào/zào	VT °make, build; create; invent; educate; go to, arrive at
崩	pēng/bēng	VT °collapse VI die (used for king or emperor)
曲	ch'ǔ/qǔ	N song, °melody; music
	ch'ǖ/qū	ADJ bent, crooked; wrong
每	měi	ADJ every, each ADV often; °on every occasion, always
奏	tsòu/zòu	VT °play (instrument); advance; present a memorial or report verbally (to the throne)
輒	ché/zhé	ADV °immediately, abruptly CONJ then
趣	ch'ǜ/qù	N interest, delight, °purport ADJ interesting, delightful
嘆	t'àn/tàn	VI sigh; admire
想	hsiǎng/xiǎng	VT think; suppose, reckon; want to N °thought
象	hsiàng/xiàng	N °image; elephant, ivory VT depict, resemble
逃	t'áo/táo	VI °run away, escape, flee; evade

Chan-kuo Ts'e 戰國策

THE *Chan-kuo ts'e* (strategies of the Warring States) is a collection of material dealing with the political, military and diplomatic events of the Warring States period which began, depending on opinion, in 481, 453 or 403 B.C. and ended in 221 B.C. when Ch'in unified China. During this period the stronger of the Chinese states were struggling to gain supremacy while the weaker ones were trying to survive. The *Chan-kuo ts'e* describes the schemes used to achieve these ends. The style is vivid and witty. Although it deals with historical events, much of the book appears to be fictitious. In its present form it was collated and edited by Liu Hsiang.

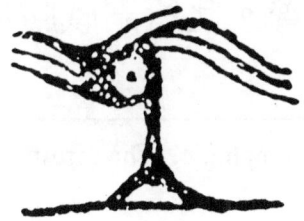

戰國策 齊策 1

鄒忌修八尺有餘，而形貌昳麗。朝服衣冠，窺鏡謂其妻曰："我孰[1]與城北徐公美？"其妻曰："君美甚。徐公何能及君也？"城北徐公，齊國之美麗者也。忌不自信而復問其妾曰："吾孰與徐公美？"妾曰："徐公何能及君也？"

且日，客從外來，與坐談。問之曰："吾與徐公孰美？"客曰："徐公不若君之美也。"

明日，徐公來。孰[2]視之，自以為不如。窺鏡而自視，又弗如遠甚。暮寢而思之，曰："吾妻之美我者，私我也。妾之美我者，畏我也。客之美我者，欲有求於我也。"

於是入朝見威王，曰："臣誠知不如徐公美。臣之妻私臣，臣之妾畏臣，臣之客欲有求於臣，皆以美於徐公。今齊地方千里，百二十城，宮婦左右，莫不私王，朝廷之臣，莫不畏王，四境之內，莫不有求於王。由此觀之，王之蔽甚矣！"王曰："善。"乃下令：群臣吏民能面刺寡人之過者，受上賞。上書諫寡人者，受中賞。能謗譏於市朝，聞寡人之耳者，受下賞。

令初下，群臣進諫，門庭若市。數月之後，時時而間進。期年之後，雖欲言，無可進者。燕趙韓魏聞之，皆朝於齊。此所謂戰勝於朝廷。

---

1 The position of 孰 is emphatic. The ordinary word order would be: 我與城北徐公孰美.

2 孰 is used here for 熟.

Vocabulary

策	ts'è/cè	N bamboo writing slip; document of appointment or dismissal from the ruler to officials; plan, °strategy; whip VT whip; record
鄒	tsōu/zōu	N °a surname; name of ancient Chinese state
忌	chì/jì	N °a proper name; taboo VT avoid; hate; be envious of VI feel (religious) dread
鄒忌	tsōu chì/zōu jì	N name of a minister of Ch'i
尺	ch'ĭh/chǐ	N °a unit of length (= 1/3 metre); ruler
貌	mào	N °appearance, manner
昳	tiéh/dié	N the setting sun
	ì/yì	See 昳麗 below
麗	lì	ADJ beautiful
昳麗	ì-lì/yìlì	ADJ handsome, beautiful
朝	ch'áo/cháo	VT summon to court VI go to court, give an audience N court, audience; dynasty
	chāo/zhāo	N °morning
冠	kuān/guān	N °cap
	kuàn/guàn	VI put on a cap
窺	k'uēi/kuī	VI °peep into, spy on
鏡	chìng/jìng	N mirror
孰	shú	INT PRON who, °which one ADV thoroughly (used for 熟)
城	ch'éng/chéng	N °city, city wall
徐	hsǘ/xú	N °a surname ADV slowly, gravely, gently
旦	tàn/dàn	N dawn, morning; day
旦日	tàn-jìh/dànrì	N the next day
客	k'ò/kè	N stranger; °guest, retainer; sojourner VT treat as a guest
暮	mù	N °evening, sunset, end of period of time
寢	ch'ĭn/qǐn	VI °sleep, rest VT stop N bedroom

私	ssū/sī	N private interest, selfishness ADJ private, personal, selfish VT °be partial to
婦	fù	N °woman; married woman, wife
廷	t'íng/tíng	N courtyard
朝廷	ch'áo-t'íng/cháotíng	N the (royal) court
蔽	pì/bì	VI be deceived VT deceive, obscure, cover N °deception
令	lìng	N °order; district magistrate; season VT cause; order, tell ADJ good, honourable
面	mièn/miàn	N face; surface; the right side; side VT face ADV °personally; directly
書	shū	N °document, letter; *Book of Documents* VT write
諫	chièn/jiàn	VT °admonish VI remonstrate N remonstration
謗	pàng/bàng	VT °censure, defame, slander
譏	chī/jī	VT °ridicule; satirize
門	mén	N °gate; family
月	yüèh/yuè	N moon, month
燕	yèn/yàn	N swallow; banquet
	yēn/yān	N °name of one of the ancient Chinese states
趙	chào/zhào	N °name of one of the ancient Chinese states; a surname
魏	wèi	N °name of one of the ancient Chinese states; a surname

戰國策 齊策 4

齊人有馮諼者。貧乏不能自存。使人屬[1]孟嘗君[2]，願寄食門下[3]。孟嘗君曰："客何好？"曰："客無好也。"曰："客何能？"曰："客無能也。"孟嘗君笑而受之曰："諾。"

左右以君賤之也，食以草具[4]。居有頃[5]，倚柱彈其劍，歌曰："長鋏歸來乎！食無魚。"左右以告。孟嘗君曰："食之比[6]門下之客。"居有頃，復彈其鋏，歌曰："長鋏歸來乎！出無車。"左右皆笑之，以告。孟嘗君曰："為之駕，比門下之車客。"於是，乘其車，揭其劍，過其友，曰："孟嘗君客我。"後有頃，復彈其劍鋏，歌曰："長鋏歸來乎！無以為家[7]。"左右皆惡之，以為貪而不知足。孟嘗君問："馮公有親乎？"對曰："有老母。"孟嘗君使人給其食用，無使乏。於是馮諼不復歌。

後孟嘗君出記，問門下諸客："誰習計會，能為文收責於薛者乎？"

馮諼署曰："能。"

---

1 屬, to entrust; here "to recommend (him) to".
2 Lord Meng-ch'ang, his name was 田文 and 孟嘗 his style.
3 門下, beneath the gate. This is a common expression to refer to those at one's gate, i.e., retainers, disciples.
4 食以草具 implies 食之以草具.
5 居有頃, stayed for a short time, i.e., after a short time.
6 比 is here used as a preposition meaning "in accordance with (the treatment), like".
7 為家, to support one's family.

孟嘗君怪之曰："此誰也？"

左右曰："乃歌夫長鋏歸來者也。"

孟嘗君笑曰："客果有能也。吾負之，未嘗見也。"

請而見之，謝曰："文倦於事，憒於憂，而性懧愚，沉於國家之事，開罪[1]於先生。先生不羞，乃有意欲為收責於薛乎？"

馮諼曰："願之。"

於是約車治裝。載券契而行。辭曰："責畢收，以何[2]市而反？"

孟嘗君曰："視吾家所寡有者。"

驅而之薛。使吏召諸民當償者悉來合券。券遍合，起，矯命以責賜諸民，因燒其券，民稱萬歲。

長驅到齊，晨而求見。孟嘗君怪其疾也，衣冠而見之，曰："責畢收乎？來何疾也！"

曰："收畢矣。"

"以何市而反？"

馮諼曰："君云：視吾家所寡有者。臣竊計，君宮中積[3]珍寶，狗馬實外廄，美人充下陳[4]；君家所寡有者以[5]義耳！竊以為君市義。"

孟嘗君曰："市義奈何？"

曰："今君有區區之薛，不拊愛子其民，因而

---

1 開罪, to commit a fault against, to offend.
2 以何 implies 以之何.
3 積 is here used as VT and means "to have accumulated", "be full of".
4 下陳 refers to the lower part of hall where gifts from host to guests and guests to host were set out.
5 以: some commentators explain it as "only", while others think it has been accidentally interpolated.

賈利之。臣竊矯君命以責賜諸民,因燒其券,民稱萬歲,乃臣所以為君市義也。"

孟嘗君不說,曰:"諾,先生休矣。"

後期年,齊王謂孟嘗君曰:"寡人不敢以先王之臣為臣。"孟嘗君就國於薛。未至百里,民扶老攜幼,迎君道中。孟嘗君顧謂馮諼:"先生所為文市義者,乃今日見之!"

馮諼曰:"狡兔有三窟,僅得免其死耳;今君有一窟,未得高枕而臥也。請為君復鑿二窟!"

孟嘗君予車五十乘,金五百斤,西遊於梁,謂惠王曰:"齊放其大臣孟嘗君於諸侯,諸侯先迎之者,富而兵強。"於是梁王虛上位,以故相為上將軍,遣使者黃金千斤,車百乘,往聘孟嘗君。馮諼先驅,誡孟嘗君曰:"千金,重幣[1]也;百乘,顯使也。齊其聞之矣。"梁使三反,孟嘗君固辭不往也。

齊王聞之,君臣恐懼。遣太傅齎黃金千斤,文車二駟,服劍一封,[2]書謝孟嘗君曰:"寡人不祥,被於宗廟之祟,沉於諂諛之臣。開罪於君!寡人不足為[3]也;願君顧先王之宗廟,姑反國統萬人乎!"馮諼誡孟嘗君曰:"願請先王之祭器,立宗廟於薛!"廟成,還報孟嘗君曰:"三窟已就,君姑高枕為樂矣!"

孟嘗君為相數十年,無纖介之禍者,馮諼之計也。

---

1 幣, a present, gift.
2 If this punctuation is correct, 封 is a measure word. It is, however, possible that the punctuation should be 一,封書 and that 封 means "sealed".
3 為, to be helped.

Vocabulary

馮	féng	N °a surname
	p'íng/píng	VI mount, ascend VT rely on; insult; ford a river
諼	hsüān	N °a proper name ADJ deceitful VI forget
貧	p'ín/pín	ADJ poor, impoverished N poverty
存	ts'ún/cún	VI be preserved; exist; survive VT °maintain, preserve
寄	chì/jì	VT send; entrust, deposit VI depend on, °become a dependent, attach oneself to
諾	nò/nuò	VI agree, "yes"
賤	chièn/jiàn	N humbleness; the humble ADJ lowly; mean, cheap, base VT °despise, humble
草	ts'ǎo/cǎo	N grass ADJ °coarse, rough
具	chǜ/jù	N what is provided (e.g., food), °provisions; implement, utensil TV prepare
頃	ch'ǐng/qǐng	ADV just; °a little while N a land measure: 100 畝
倚	ǐ/yǐ	VI °lean on, rest against; rely on ADJ biased, partial
柱	chù/zhù	N pillar, column VT support
彈	t'án/tán	VT °tap, pluck (an instrument); flick; accuse VI spring
	tàn/dàn	N pellet, bullet
劍	chièn/jiàn	N °sword VT kill with sword
歌	kō/gē	N song VT & VI °sing
鋏	chiá/jiá	N °sword; hilt of sword
駕	chià/jià	VT °yoke or drive a carriage; ride in N carriage
揭	chiēh/jiē	VT lift off, uncover; raise, °hold up in the air; make known
貪	t'ān/tān	VT covet ADJ corrupt; °greedy

給	chǐ/jǐ	VT °supply, provide; grant ADJ well-provided, ample
計	chì/jì	N plan; idea VT calculate, estimate; plan for
會	k'uài/kuài	N calculation VI calculate
	huì	VI collect together, assemble, meet N opportunity, meeting
計會	chì-k'uài/jìkuài	N °accounting; book-keeper, accountant (often written 會計)
收	shōu	VT °collect; receive; accept; gather
責	chài/zhài	N °debt (also written 債)
	tsé/zé	VT demand; blame, reprove N duty, responsibility
薛	hsüēh/xuē	N name of Meng-ch'ang's fief in Ch'i
署	shǔ	VT arrange; °sign; act as deputy N office
怪	kuài/guài	ADJ extraordinary, strange VT °surprised at, treat as strange; blame
謝	hsièh/xiè	VT thank; °apologize; decline (an offer etc.) VI wither
倦	chüàn/juàn	ADJ weary, tired
憒	k'uèi/kuì	ADJ disturbed, muddle-headed VI °be disturbed
憂	yū/yōu	VI worry, be worried N sorrow, °anxiety
懧	nò/nuò	ADJ cowardly; °weak, timid
愚	yǘ/yú	ADJ °stupid, foolish, simple-minded VT fool, make a fool of
沉	ch'én/chén	VI °be submerged in, sink; wallow, indulge ADJ deep; heavy
開	k'āi/kāi	VT °open; begin; develop
約	yüēh/yuē	VT restrain, bind; agree to do; invite; °order, make arrangements for N agreement, treaty
裝	chuāng/zhuāng	N °baggage VT pretend, feign, make believe; dress up, attire; pack; load
載	tsài/zài	VT °load, contain, carry or transport (by vessel or cart)
	tsǎi/zǎi	N year VT record

券	ch'üàn/quàn	N a contract made up of two parts of which each party takes one
契	ch'ì/qì	N °contract, deed VT engrave, carve (also written 契); agree
畢	pì/bì	VI be finished, complete ADV °completely, entirely
召	chào/zhào	VT call, summon
償	ch'áng/cháng	VT °repay, compensate; fulfil
悉	hsī/xī	ADV °all, entirely VT know, learn
矯	chiǎo/jiǎo	VT reform, correct, straighten out; falsify, °feign ADJ strong, brave
燒	shāo	VT °burn; cook; run a fever N fever
稱	ch'ēng/chēng	VT °call, address; state; praise; weigh
	ch'èng/chèng	N balance, steelyard (also written 秤)
	ch'èn/chèn	VT suit, agree with, match
到	tào/dào	VT arrive, reach; °go to, leave for ADV up to, until
晨	ch'én/chén	N morning
竊	ch'ièh/qiè	VT steal ADV stealthily, furtively. Expression used to refer to oneself when addressing superiors: I venture to, I presume to
積	chī/jī	N accumulation VI collect, °accumulate
珍	chēn/zhēn	N °treasure ADJ precious, rare VT treasure
廄	chiù/jiù	N stable
陳	ch'én/chén	VT set out, spread out; put on display; state ADJ old, stale N corridor from the main hall to the gate
奈	nài	VT deal with, do something about someone or something, remedy
奈何	nài-hó/nàihé	what can be done; °in what way
區	ch'ū/qū	N area, region VT distinguish, classify
區區	ch'ū-ch'ū/qūqū	ADJ °trivial, trifling
拊	fǔ	VT °comfort, console; foster; stroke; clap
賈	kǔ/gǔ	N °merchant VT trade; bring about

	chià/jià	N price (also written 價)
休	hsiū/xiū	VT °desist, cease, stop; cast off (one's wife) N good fortune; happiness ADV do not
扶	fú	VT °support, assist, prop up
攜	hsié/xié	VT carry, °lead by the hand
迎	yíng	VT go to meet, greet, °welcome
狡	chiǎo/jiǎo	ADJ crafty, °cunning
窟	k'ū/kū	N hole, cave; °den
僅	chǐn/jǐn	ADV merely, °barely, only
	chìn/jìn	ADV almost
枕	chěn/zhěn	N pillow VT °rest head on
臥	wò	VI °lie down, rest
鑿	tsáo/záo	VT °chisel, cut a hole N chisel
	tsuò/zuò	ADJ clear; definite
金	chīn/jīn	N metal, °gold; money ADJ golden, precious
放	fàng	VT °banish; loosen, let go; indulge
侯	hóu	N °feudal lord; marquis
虛	hsū̄/xū	N falseness, hollowness ADJ empty, false, illusory VT °make vacant
軍	chūn/jūn	N army, camp VI encamp
上將軍	shàng-chiāng-chūn/shàngjiāng-jūn	N commander-in-chief
遣	ch'iěn/qiǎn	VT °send, dispatch; expel, banish
黃	huáng	N yellow ADJ °yellow, sallow
聘	p'ìn/pìn	VT betroth; °invite to take up appointment (often with gifts); inquire after
誡	chièh/jiè	VT °warn, admonish N commandment
恐	k'ǔng/kǒng	VI be afraid
懼	chǜ/jù	VI be afraid VT fear, dread
傅	fù	VT teach, instruct; apply, add; assist N teacher

太傅	t'ài-fù/tàifù	N title of high official in ancient China
齎	chī/jī	VT °give a gift; carry, grasp
駟	ssù/sì	N team of four horses
封	fēng	N fief, boundary; mound VT enfeoff; seal
祥	hsiáng/xiáng	ADJ °lucky, auspicious, propitious
被	pèi/bèi	N quilt AUX used in front of verb to make it passive VT be covered by; °suffer
宗	tsūng/zōng	N °ancestor; clan; sect; principal aim; model VT take as model
廟	miào	N temple, shrine
宗廟	tsūng-miào/zōngmiào	N ancestral temple
祟	suì	N °evil spirit, evil influence; calamity
諂	ch'ǎn/chǎn	VT °flatter VI fawn on
諛	yǘ/yú	VT °flatter ADJ flattering
姑	kū/gū	N girl, maiden; paternal aunt ADV °for the time being
統	t'ǔng/tǒng	N system; end of thread on cocoon; clue VT gather into one, unite, conduct; °govern, rule ADV all, together
器	ch'ì/qì	N °implement, vessel; organ; capacity, talent
成	ch'éng/chéng	VI °be completed VT complete, perfect, succeed
報	pào/bào	VT °inform, report to, announce to; repay N retribution, report
樂	lò/lè	ADJ happy N °happiness, joy VT be happy
	yüèh/yuè	N music
纖	hsiēn/xiān	ADJ °fine, minute
介	chièh/jiè	VI be situated between, border on VT protect; assist; enlarge ADJ resolute, upright; °small N armour, shell; border ADV alone
禍	huò	N °calamity, misfortune, disaster ADJ calamitous

戰國策　楚策 1

荊宣王[1]問群臣曰："吾聞北方之畏昭奚恤[2]也。果誠何如？"

群臣莫對。江一對曰："虎求百獸而食之。得狐，狐曰：'子無敢食我也。天帝使我長百獸。今子食我，是逆天帝命也。子以我為不信，吾為子先行，子隨我後，觀百獸之見我而敢不走乎！'虎以為然。故遂與之行。獸見之皆走。虎不知獸畏己而走也，以為畏狐也。今王之地方五千里，帶甲[3]百萬，而專屬之昭奚恤。故北方之畏奚恤也，其實畏王之甲兵也，猶百獸之畏虎也。"

1　Ascended the throne in 370 B.C.
2　昭奚恤 Chao Hsi-hsü, a general of Ch'u.
3　帶甲, soldiers wearing armour, armoured soldiers.

Vocabulary

荊	chīng/jīng	N chaste tree; thorn, bramble; °another name for 楚
昭	chāo/zhāo	N brightness; °a surname ADJ bright VT show, display
恤	hsǜ/xù	N worry, anxiety; °a proper name VI & VT worry; sympathize; compensate
狐	hú	N fox
帝	tì/dì	N °the supreme being; emperor
逆	nì	VT go against, °disobey ADJ contrary N traitor
隨	suí	VT °follow VI comply with, adapt to
專	chuān/zhuān	ADV °only, solely VI act on one's own responsibility

Hsün-tzu 荀子

Hsün K'uang 荀況 (c.313-c.238 B.C.) was more often called Hsün Ch'ing 荀卿. Like Mencius before him, he travelled widely, was unsuccessful in political life and became a teacher of note. The basic texts he used in his teaching were the Chinese Classics: the *Book of Documents*, the *Book of Songs*, the *Book of Rites*, the *Spring and Autumn Annals*, etc. Also like Mencius before him he was a transmitter of Confucian ethics, but unlike Mencius who made goodness and righteousness the basis of his political philosophy, Hsün-tzu placed particular stress on the rites and on law and education. He was strongly opposed to any form of superstition and argued for a realistic and naturalistic view of the universe and of man.

Hsün-tzu's writings consist of a series of essays, each with a title indicating the theme. The essays are logically structured and clearly argued, very different from the dialogue-style of the *Mencius*. The *Hsün-tzu* appears to have been well preserved and the length of the text is consistent with what early records tell us. In general, most scholars regard it as a genuine work.

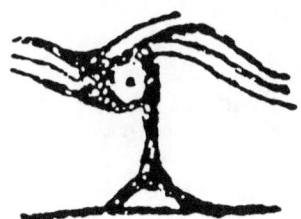

荀子　勸學 c.1

君子曰："學不可以已[1]。"青，取之於藍，而青於藍；冰，水為之，而寒於水。木直中繩，輮以為輪，其曲中規。雖有槁暴[2]，不復挺者，輮使之然也。故木受繩則直，金就礪則利，君子博學而日參省乎己，則知明而行無過矣。

故不登高山，不知天之高也；不臨深谿，不知地之厚也；不聞先王之遺言，不知學問之大也。干越夷貉之子，生而同聲，長而異俗，教使之然也。詩[3]曰："嗟爾君子，無恆安息。靖共爾位，好是正直。神之聽之，介爾景福"。神莫大於化道[4]，福莫長於無禍。

吾嘗終日而思矣，不如須臾之所學也；吾嘗跂而望矣，不如登高之博見也。登高而招，臂非加長也，而見者遠；順風而呼，聲非加疾[5]也，而聞者彰。假輿馬者，非利足[6]也，而致千里；假舟楫者，非能水[7]也，而絕江河。君子生非異也，善假於物也。

1　已, to end, finish.
2　暴, to dry in the sun.
3　*Song* 207.
4　化道, to transform oneself with the Way.
5　疾, sharp (of voice).
6　利足, good, strong legs.
7　能水, skilled in water.

南方有鳥焉，名曰蒙鳩。以羽為巢，而編之以髮，繫之葦苕。風至苕折，卵破子死。巢非不完也，所繫者然也。西方有木焉，名曰射干。莖長四寸。生於高山之上，而臨百仞之淵。木莖非能長也，所立者然也。蓬生麻中，不扶而直。蘭槐之根是為芷。其漸之滫，君子不近，庶人不服。其質非不美也，所漸者然也。故君子居必擇鄉，遊必就士，所以防邪僻而近中正也。

Vocabulary

荀	hsűn/xún	N °a surname; a mythological plant
勸	ch'üàn/quàn	VT °encourage, urge, persuade
青	ch'īng/qīng	N °blue, green, black; colour of nature ADJ blue, green, black
藍	lán	N °indigo plant, blue
冰	pīng/bīng	N °ice, frost ADJ pure
繩	shéng	N cord, rope; °plumb-line, marking-line; a normal standard VT measure; correct
輮	jóu/róu	N the periphery of a wheel VT °bend (used for 揉)
輪	lún	N °wheel; circular object VT take turns
規	kuēi/guī	N °compass, rule, law VT admonish; plan
槁	kǎo/gǎo	VT wither; °dry
挺	t'ǐng/tǐng	VI °straighten; endure VT draw out, pull up; straighten ADJ straight, erect
礪	lì	N °whetstone VT whet, sharpen
博	pó/bó	VT °broaden; win, gain ADJ broad, extensive; abundant
參	shēn	N ginseng; name of star
	sān	N three
	ts'ān/cān	VT join in; consult; refer; visit to pay one's respects to; impeach; °examine
	ts'ēn/cēn	ADJ irregular, uneven
臨	lín	VT °approach, be near to VI look down from a high place
谿	hsī/xī	N °mountain stream, brook (also written 溪, and also pronounced ch'ī/qī)
干	kān/gān	VT offend; seek; involve N bank; rod (used for 竿); shield
	hán	N °an ancient Chinese state (used for 邗)
越	yüèh/yuè	N °name of one of the ancient Chinese states VT transgress, exceed, cross over

夷	í/yí	N °non-Chinese tribes (especially those from the east) ADJ level, even
貉	hó/hé	N racoon dog
	mò	N °northeastern tribe (used for 貉)
俗	sú	N °customs ADJ rustic, vulgar, common
嗟	chüēh/juē	N an interjection: oh! alas! (also pronounced *chiēh/jiē*) VI sigh with feeling
恆	héng	ADJ °constant, lasting; regular ADV constantly
息	hsī/xī	VI grow; breathe; rest, stop, °be at rest N breath
靖	chìng/jìng	VT cease; pacify, settle ADJ respectful, °thoughtful
共	kùng/gòng	ADJ whole ADV together, jointly
	kūng/gōng	ADJ °respectful (used for 恭)
神	shén	ADJ spiritual, divine; magical N °spirit, god; expression, mind
景	chǐng/jǐng	N sunlight; view, prospect; circumstances ADJ °great, high
福	fú	N good fortune, blessing
須	hsū/xū	VT wait; need V AUX must, have to, should N beard; need
須臾	hsū-yú/xūyú	N moment, instant
跂	ch'ì/qì	VT stand on tiptoe
招	chāo/zhāo	VI °wave arms VT call, beckon
臂	pì/bì	N °arm, upper arm
順	shùn	VI be attuned VT °follow, accord with; obey ADJ suitable, agreeable; compliant
彰	chāng/zhāng	ADJ °clear, evident, conspicuous VT display; clear
假	chiǎ/jiǎ	ADJ false, artificial VT °borrow PREP supposing
舟	chōu/zhōu	N boat

楫	chí/jí	N °oar VT row; compile (used for 輯)
鳥	niǎo	N bird
蒙	méng	N dodder; depreciatory term for oneself: I, my VT cover; meet with; cheat; receive ADJ gloomy; dull
鳩	chiū/jiū	N pigeon
蒙鳩	méng-chiū/ méngjiū	N a finch-like bird
編	piēn/biān	N leather strip used to tie bamboo slips in ancient times VT °weave; arrange in order
髮	fà	N hair
繫	hsì/xì	VT °attach, tie, fasten; involve, concern; constrain; arrest
葦	wěi	N reed
苕	t'iáo/tiáo	N reed flower; a kind of grass
葦苕	wěi-t'iáo/wěitiáo	N reed flower
卵	luǎn	N egg
破	p'ò/pò	VI °break, split; destroy; defeat VT smash, break ADJ broken, damaged
完	wán	ADJ °intact, whole; solid VT finish; preserve; renovate; strengthen N a light punishment in ancient times
射	shè	VT shoot; pursue; guess N archery
	yèh/yè	N see 射干 below
射干	yèh-kàn/yègàn	N *Belamcanda chinensis* (a kind of small plant); blackberry lily
莖	chīng/jīng	N stem (of a plant), °stalk; handle
寸	ts'ùn/cùn	N °a unit of length, an inch ADJ little, small
仞	jèn/rèn	N °measure of eight feet VT measure
淵	yüān/yuān	N °deep pool ADJ deep
蓬	p'éng/péng	N °thistle ADJ overgrown, tangled, dishevelled

麻	má	N °hemp; hempen mourning garment; special term for imperial edicts in the T'ang and Sung dynasties
蘭	lán	N orchid; lily magnolia; fence (used for 欄) ADJ bright-coloured (used for 爛)
槐	huái	N Chinese scholar tree
蘭槐	lán-huái	N Eumenol angelica
根	kēn/gēn	N °root; base, foundation; beginning
芷	chǐh/zhǐ	N Eumenol angelica
漸	chièn/jiàn	ADV gradually, by degrees VT aggravate
	chiēn/jiān	VI flow VT °soak, wet
滫	hsiū/xiū	N °water in which rice has been washed; urine
質	chìh/zhì	N nature; quality; °substance, matter; pledge; target; object VT interrogate; pledge
防	fáng	VT °guard against N embankment, dike
邪	hsiéh/xié	ADJ °depraved, crooked
	yéh/yé	PART final interrogative particle
僻	p'ì/pì	ADJ °low, rustic, secluded; eccentric; rare

Chuang-tzu 莊子

CHUANG Chou 莊周 was a contemporary of Mencius. He is said to have held a minor post for a brief period but he gave it up to live in retirement. Even less is known of his life than of the life of the other philosophers of this period. Most of the "information" comes from anecdotes about him which have been recorded in the book that bears his name. How much of this is true and how much is legend is impossible to say; however, a very colourful individual emerges, one who scorns honour and wealth and believes in the transience of all things.

The *Chuang-tzu* has been traditionally ascribed to Chuang Chou. However, the extant text is not homogenous. The seven "inner chapters" are regarded as the work of Chuang Chou and contain the main themes of his philosophy. The rest of the book is fairly miscellaneous though some parts may have been written by Chuang Chou; there are some sections that are thought to have been composed by his followers, and some from other Taoist schools; some sections are thought to be collections of fragments.

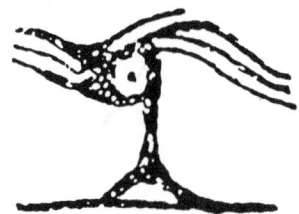

莊子 山木 c.20

　　莊子行於山中，見大木，枝葉盛茂，伐木者止其旁而不取也。問其故，曰："無所可用。"莊子曰："此木以不材得終其天年。"夫子出於山，舍於故人之家。故人喜，命豎子殺雁而烹之。豎子請曰："其一能鳴，其一不能鳴，請奚殺？"主人曰："殺不能鳴者。"明日，弟子問於莊子曰："昨日山中之木，以不材得終其天年，今主人之雁，以不材死；先生將何處[1]？"莊子笑曰："周[2]將處乎材與不材之間。材與不材之間，似之[3]而非也，故未免乎累。若夫乘道德而浮遊，則不然，無譽無訾，一龍一蛇，與時俱化，而無肯專為[4]；一上一下，以和為量，浮遊乎萬物之祖，物物[5]而不物於物，則胡可得而累邪！此神農、黃帝[6]之法則也。若夫萬物之情，人倫之傳，則不然。合則離，成則毀，廉則挫，尊則議，有為則虧，賢則謀，不肖則欺，胡可得而必乎哉！悲夫！弟子志之，其唯道德之鄉乎！"

1　處, to take a position, view.
2　周 is the given name of Chuang-tzu.
3　之, it, here refers to the right way, the right thing to do.
4　專為, to be/do one thing alone.
5　物物: V + OBJ to treat things as things.
6　神農、黃帝, Shen-nung and Huang-ti. Legendary sage rulers. Shen-nung is said to have invented the plough and to have taught people about agriculture; he was the first to experiment with the healing properties of plants. Huang-ti or the Yellow Emperor is also connected with farming (yellow is the colour of the earth), and he is said to have taught people to plant grain, plants and trees and to domesticate animals. In some accounts he is said to have invented the state.

Vocabulary

莊	chuāng/zhuāng	ADJ grave, serious N °a surname; dignity; village; manor
盛	shèng	ADJ full, °abundant
	ch'éng/chéng	VT fill, put into (container)
茂	mào	ADJ exuberant; rich and splendid, °luxuriant
旁	p'áng/páng	ADV by the side of; widespread N °side
	pàng/bàng	VT depend on (also written 傍)
喜	hsǐ/xǐ	VT like, delight in VI °be pleased, rejoice
豎	shù	N °servant VT set up, establish
雁	yèn/yàn	N wild goose, °goose (used for 鵝 ó/é)
烹	p'ēng/pēng	VT boil, °cook; fry
鳴	míng	N cry of birds, animals and insects VI ring, sound, °cry, call VT express
昨	tsó/zuó	N °yesterday ADV lately
間	chiēn/jiān	PW among, °between
	chièn/jiàn	VT separate, divide VI come between; find fault with ADV intermittently
累	lèi	VI °be bound VT implicate; trouble; tire N burden, troubles
	lěi	VT accumulate
浮	fú	VI °float, drift ADJ light, volatile, insubstantial ADV excessive
訾	tzǔ/zǐ	VT slander N °slander
龍	lúng/lóng	N dragon
俱	chǜ/jù	ADV all, in both cases, completely; °together
肯	k'ěn/kěn	V AUX be willing to
量	liáng	VT measure N °measurement

	liàng	N capacity, quantity, amount VT estimate
祖	tsǔ/zǔ	N °ancestor, grandfather; origin, beginning
情	ch'íng/qíng	N feelings; facts of case, °facts
倫	lún	N °human relationship, moral obligations ADJ constant, regular
毀	huǐ	VT destroy, ruin; defame; burn up VI °be destroyed
廉	lién/lián	N °honesty ADJ honest, upright; low-priced, cheap
挫	ts'ò/cuò	VT defeat; push down, grind VI °suffer defeat; be frustrated
議	ì/yì	N counsel, agreement VT discuss, consult; reproach; °censure, criticize VI deliberate
虧	k'uēi/kuī	VT have a deficit; lack; fail VI °suffer failure; diminish ADJ deficient, short of, lacking in ADV fortunately, luckily
謀	móu	N plan, plot VT plan; °plot
肖	hsiào/xiào	VT resemble, be like
	hsiāo/xiāo	N decline (used for 消)
不肖	pú-hsiào/búxiào	ADJ unworthy, unfilial
欺	ch'ī/qī	VT deceive, cheat
唯	wéi	ADV °only (also written 惟)
	wěi	PART yes (predicate substitute)

莊子 徐無鬼 c.24

莊子送葬，過惠子[1]之墓，顧謂從者曰："郢人堊慢其鼻端，若蠅翼，使匠石[2]斲之。匠石運斤成風，聽而斲之，盡堊而鼻不傷，郢人立不失容。宋元君聞之，召匠石曰：'嘗試為寡人為之。'匠石曰：'臣則嘗能斲之。雖然，臣之質死久矣。'自夫子之死也，吾無以為質矣！吾無與言之矣。"

莊子 秋水 c.17

莊子釣於濮水，楚王使大夫二人往先焉，曰："願以境內累矣！"莊子持竿不顧，曰："吾聞楚有神龜，死已三千歲矣；王巾笥而藏之廟堂之上。此龜者，寧其死為留骨而貴乎？寧其生而曳尾於塗中乎？"二大夫曰："寧生而曳尾塗中。"莊子曰："往矣！吾將曳尾於塗中。"

---

1 惠子, Master Hui, his given name was Shih 施. He was a sophist. Chuang-tzu may have been his disciple; if this is true, he soon turned from the analytical study of paradoxes to a study of the spontaneous and natural. The two, however, remained firm friends and several discussions between the two are recorded in the *Chuang-tzu*.

2 石 is the name of the artisan.

Vocabulary

鬼	kuěi/guǐ	N °a proper name; ghost, spirit of the dead
送	sùng/sòng	VT deliver, carry; °escort, see off; give (as gift)
葬	tsàng/zàng	VT bury, inter N °funeral
墓	mù	N tomb, grave
郢	yǐng	N capital of the state of Ch'u
堊	ò/è	N °plaster, chalk VT whitewash
慢	màn	ADJ slow; supercilious; neglectful VT postpone; brim over; °cover (used for 漫)
鼻	pí/bí	N nose
蠅	yíng	N fly
翼	ì/yì	N °wing VT assist, shelter
匠	chiàng/jiàng	N °artisan, craftsman
斲	chó/zhuó	VI °slice off, hack off, chop, hew
容	júng/róng	N °facial expression; appearance, looks VT hold, contain; permit, allow
元	yüán/yuán	ADJ °first, primary; basic; chief
久	chiǔ/jiǔ	ADJ °long time ADV for a long time
釣	tiào/diào	VI °angle, fish
濮	p'ú/pú	N °name of a river; a tribe in the south-west
竿	kān/gān	N pole; °rod
龜	kuēi/guī	N °turtle, tortoise
巾	chīn/jīn	N a piece of cloth used as a towel, scarf, kerchief
笥	ssù/sì	N bamboo-plaited basket or box
巾笥	chīn-ssù/jīnsì	VI wrap something in cloth and place it in a box
藏	ts'áng/cáng	VI °store, hoard, hide
	tsàng/zàng	N storehouse; Buddhist and Taoist canons
留	liú	VI remain, stay VT detain; °preserve, save; leave
骨	kǔ/gǔ	N °bone, skeleton; framework
尾	wěi	N °tail; end; remaining part
	ì/yǐ	N hair of horse's tail, spikelet on cricket's tail

莊子　秋水　c.17

惠子相梁，莊子往見之。或謂惠子曰："莊子來，欲代子相。"於是惠子恐，搜於國中，三日三夜。莊子往見之，曰："南方有鳥，其名為鵷鶵，子知之乎？夫鵷鶵，發於南海，而飛於北海；非梧桐不止，非練實不食，非醴泉不飲。於是鴟得腐鼠，鵷鶵過之，仰而視之曰：'嚇！'今子欲以子之梁國而嚇我邪？"

莊子　秋水　c.17

莊子與惠子遊於濠梁之上。莊子曰："儵魚出遊從容，是魚之樂也。"

惠子曰："子非魚。安知魚之樂？"

莊子曰："子非我。安知我不知魚之樂？"

惠子曰："我非子，固不知子矣。子固非魚也。子之不知魚之樂全矣。"

莊子曰："請循其本。子曰：'汝安知魚樂'云者。既已知吾知之而問我。我知之濠上也。"

Vocabulary

代	tài/dài	VT °take the place of VI alternate N generation, dynasty
搜	sōu	VI & VT °search; ransack
鵷鶵	yüān-ch'ú/yuānchú	N legendary bird similar to phoenix
飛	fēi	VI °fly, hover (in air) ADJ unexpected, accidental ADV swiftly
梧桐	wú-t'úng/wútóng	N Chinese parasol tree (*Firmiana simplex*)
練	lièn/liàn	VT select; practise, train; soften and whiten raw silk by boiling N white silk ADJ experienced
練實	lièn-shíh/liànshí	N bamboo seed
醴	lǐ	N sweet rice wine; °sweet spring water
鴟	ch'īh/chī	N °hawk, kite; owl
腐	fǔ	ADJ °rotten, putrid, stale
鼠	shǔ	N rat, mouse
嚇	hò/hè	N °exclamation of anger or dissatisfaction
	hsià/xià	VT open out; intimidate, frighten
濠	háo	N °name of a river; city moat
鯈	ch'óu/chóu	N a white fish, minnow (also pronounced *yú/yóu*)
從容	ts'úng-júng/cóngróng	ADJ calm, unhurried, free and easy
全	ch'üán/quán	ADJ complete, whole, entire ADV entirely, completely VT make perfect VI °be complete, perfect
循	hsűn/xún	VT °follow, trace back; comply with ADV orderly, step by step
汝	jǔ/rǔ	PRON second person pronoun: you (used when speaking to those with whom one is on intimate terms or to inferiors)

莊子 養生主 c.3

庖丁[1]為文惠君解牛，手之所觸，肩之所倚，足之所履，膝之所踦，砉然嚮然，奏刀[2]騞然，莫不中音。合於桑林[3]之舞，乃中經首[4]之會。文惠君曰："譆，善哉！技蓋至此乎？"

庖丁釋刀對曰："臣之所好者，道也。進乎技矣。始臣之解牛之時，所見無非牛者。三年之後，未嘗見全牛也。方今之時，臣以神遇，而不以目視。官知止而神欲行。依乎天理。批大郤，導大窾，因其固然。技經肯綮之未嘗，而況大軱乎！良庖歲更刀，割也。族庖月更刀，折也。今臣之刀，十九年矣，所解數千牛矣，而刀刃若新發於硎。彼節者有閒，而刀刃者無厚。以無厚入有閒，恢恢乎，其於遊刃必有餘地矣。是以十九年而刀刃若新發於硎。雖然，每至於族，吾見其難為。怵然為戒，視為止，行為遲。動刀甚微，謋然已解，如土委地。提刀而立，為之四顧，為之躊躇滿志[5]。善刀而藏之。"

文惠君曰："善哉！吾聞庖丁之言，得養生焉。"

---

1 Some commentators say that Ting 丁 is a given name.
2 奏刀, to brandish a knife.
3 桑林, Mulberry Forest, name of a tune which traditionally came from the Shang dynasty.
4 經首, name of a tune which according to legend comes from the time of Emperor Yao.
5 躊躇滿志, complacent and satisfied.

Vocabulary

丁	tīng/dīng	N man; member of a family; °person engaged in certain occupation; fourth of the ten heavenly stems
庖丁	p'áo-tīng/ páodīng	N cook
解	chiěh/jiě	VT °cut up; relieve, loosen, untie; release; explain
手	shǒu	N hand
肩	chiēn/jiān	N °shoulder VI take on (responsibility or burden)
膝	hsī/xī	N knee
踦	ǐ/yǐ	VT °prop up
	ch'ī/qī	ADJ one-legged, crippled
	chī/jī	ADJ single
砉	hsū/xū	N sound of flesh separating from bone
嚮	hsiǎng/xiǎng	VT °make a noise (used for 響)
	hsiàng/xiàng	N window facing north; direction VT face VI be close to ADV formerly, before, in the past
刀	tāo/dāo	N knife
騞	huō	N sound of knife cutting flesh
舞	wǔ	N °dance VT & VI dance; brandish
經	chīng/jīng	N warp of fabric; invariable rule; a classic book VT pass through; arrange, plan
首	shǒu	N head; first; chief; direction VT confess guilt
譆	hsī/xī	N exclamation of praise and admiration (also written 嘻)
技	chì/jì	N °skill, ability; artisan
蓋	hó/hé	INT ADV why, why not; °how (usually written 盍)
	kài/gài	VT cover, conceal N canopy PART initial particle indicating probability: I suppose CONJ for, now
遇	yǜ/yù	VT °meet; entertain VI get along

目	mù	N °eye; item VT regard
官	kuān/guān	N °the senses; official, public office
依	ī/yī	VI rely on, depend on; °comply with N support ADV according to
批	p'ī/pī	VT slap, °strike; get rid of; pare
郤	hsì/xì	N °crack, gap (used for 隙)
窾	k'uǎn/kuǎn	N °hollow
技經	chì-chīng/jìjīng	N vein
綮	ch'ǐ/qǐ	N sinew
肯綮	k'ěn-ch'ǐ/kěnqǐ	N tendon
況	k'uàng/kuàng	N condition, situation VT compare ADV moreover; °how much the more/less
軱	kū/gū	N large bone
割	kō/gē	VT cut
族	tsú/zú	N clan; °class, species; extermination of whole family
硎	hsíng/xíng	N whetstone
恢	huī	ADJ extensive; °vast VT expand
遲	ch'íh/chí	ADJ late, slow ADV °slowly
動	tùng/dòng	VT °move VI move; start; take action, rouse N movement
微	wēi	NEG ADV not (used like 無), if it were not, unless (used like 非) ADJ °slight, minute; mean; humble, obscure ADV slightly
謋	huò	N sound of flesh being separated from bone
委	wěi	VT entrust, appoint; throw away, give up; °pile up ADJ crooked; withered (used for 萎) ADV actually, really
提	t'í/tí	VT °hold in the hand; lift; promote
躊躇	ch'óu-ch'ú/chóuchú	VI hesitate; stop; °be self-satisfied
滿	mǎn	VT fill VI be full; °be satisfied ADJ whole

莊子 逍遙遊 c.1

北冥有魚，其名為鯤。鯤之大，不知其幾千里也；化而為鳥，其名為鵬。鵬之背，不知其幾千里也；怒而飛，其翼若垂天之雲。是鳥也，海運則將徙於南冥。南冥者，天池也。齊諧[1]者，志怪[2]者也。諧之言曰："鵬之徙於南冥也，水擊三千里，摶扶搖而上者九萬里，去以六月息者也。"野馬也，塵埃也，生物之以息相吹也。天之蒼蒼，其正色邪，其遠而無所至極邪？其視下也，亦若是則已矣。且夫水之積也不厚，則其負大舟也無力。覆杯水於坳堂[3]之上，則芥為之舟，置杯焉則膠，水淺而舟大也。風之積也不厚，則其負大翼也無力。故九萬里則風斯在下矣，而後乃今培風；背負青天而莫之夭閼者，而後乃今將圖南。蜩與學鳩笑之曰："我決起而飛，槍榆枋，時則不至，而控於地而已矣。奚以之九萬里而南為！"適莽蒼者，三餐而反，腹猶果然；適百里者，宿舂糧；適千里者，三月聚糧。之二蟲，又何知！小知不及大知，小年不及大年。奚以知其然也？朝菌不知晦朔，蟪蛄不知春秋：此小年也。楚之南有冥靈[4]者，以五百歲為春，五百歲為秋；上古有大椿者，以八千歲為春，八千歲為秋。而彭

---

1 齊諧, name of a book, the *Fables of Ch'i*.
2 志怪, record of marvels; a generic name given to stories about extraordinary people and events.
3 坳堂, hole in floor.
4 冥靈, name of a tree.

祖¹乃今以久特聞，眾人匹之，不亦悲乎？

湯之問棘²也是已。窮髮之北，有冥海者，天池也。有魚焉，其廣數千里，未有知其修者，其名為鯤。有鳥焉，其名為鵬，背若泰山，翼若垂天之雲；搏扶搖羊角³而上者九萬里，絕雲氣，負青天，然後圖南，且適南冥也。斥鴳笑之，曰："彼且奚適也！我騰躍而上，不過數仞而下，翱翔蓬蒿之間，此亦飛之至也。而彼且奚適也！"此小大之辯也。

1　彭祖, P'eng-tsu, legendary person said to have lived 800 years.
2　棘, Chi, a wise man who became minister to Emperor T'ang.
3　羊角, ram's horn, i.e., [to ascend] in a spiral.

Vocabulary

逍	hsiāo/xiāo	VI ramble, wander
遙	yáo	ADJ distant, remote, long
逍遙	hsiāo-yáo/xiāoyáo	ADV leisurely
冥	míng	N °sea, ocean ADJ deep, profound, dark
鯤	k'ūn/kūn	N name of a large fish
鵬	p'éng/péng	N name of a large bird
背	pèi/bèi	N °back VT turn one's back on, revolt; recite ADV back to back
	pēi/bēi	VT carry on the back
怒	nù	VI °put forth effort; be angry ADJ angry
垂	ch'uí/chuí	VT °hang from, bring down; hand down
雲	yǘn/yún	N cloud
徙	hsǐ/xǐ	VI °set out, go VT move (house)
諧	hsiéh/xié	N °fable VI harmonize, accord with
擊	chī/jī	VT hit, °strike, kill, attack
摶	t'uán/tuán	VT °turn, roll round
搖	yáo	VT shake, wave
扶搖	fú-yáo	N whirlwind
野	yěh/yě	N uncultivated fields, open country ADJ rustic, wild
野馬	yěh-mǎ/yěmǎ	N °heat-haze; fine horse bred in Northern China
塵	ch'én/chén	N dust, floating dust
埃	āi	N dust, dirt
吹	ch'uī/chuī	VT °blow VI blow
蒼	ts'āng/cāng	N & ADJ °azure, green, grey
色	sè	N °colour; appearance; beauty
極	chí/jí	N °extreme limit; ridge-pole VT exhaust ADV very, greatly
覆	fù	VT °overturn; defeat; repeat; cover over

杯	pēi/bēi	N cup
坳	āo	N hollow in ground
芥	chièh/jiè	N °seed, small plant; mustard plant
膠	chiāo/jiāo	VT °stick, stick to N glue
淺	ch'iěn/qiǎn	ADJ °shallow, light, simple
培	p'éi/péi	VT bank up (earth)
培風	p'éi-fēng/péifēng	V + OBJ ride the wind, 培 used for 憑 *p'íng/píng*
夭	yāo	VI die prematurely VT °cut off
閼	ò/è	VT °obstruct, stop
圖	t'ú/tú	N chart; picture, plan VT °plan; consider
蜩	t'iáo/tiáo	N cicada
學鳩	hsüéh-chiū/xuéjiū	N finch
槍	ch'iāng/qiāng	N spear VT °run against (also written 搶)
榆	yű/yú	N elm tree
枋	fāng	N sandalwood tree
控	k'ùng/kòng	VI draw back, °fall VT draw (a bow); control; accuse, inform
莽	mǎng	N undergrowth, jungle, dense vegetation ADJ disorderly, rough
莽蒼	mǎng-ts'āng/mǎngcāng	N °blueness of wide spaces; countryside
餐	ts'ān/cān	N °meal VT eat
宿	sù	VI °stay the night, lodge overnight N halting place ADJ old ADV in the past
	hsiù/xiù	N constellation
舂	ch'ūng/chōng	VT pound (e.g., grain to remove husks or herbs for medicine)
糧	liáng	N °provisions, grain, food; taxes in kind
聚	chǜ/jù	VT °gather, collect, assemble
菌	chǜn/jùn	N mushroom

晦	huì	N °last phase of moon ADJ obscure, dark
朔	shuò	N °first phase of moon ADJ northern
蟪蛄	huì-kū/huìgū	N cicada, cricket
靈	líng	N spirit, divine; intelligence ADJ supernatural, spiritual
椿	ch'ūn/chūn	N name of a tree
彭	p'éng/péng	N °a surname, place name ADJ proud
特	t'è/tè	ADJ special, alone; unique ADV °specially N a male animal
匹	p'ǐ/pǐ	N mate, one of a pair VT °match ADJ single MW for horse, roll of silk
棘	chí/jí	N °a name; jujube tree
窮髮	ch'iúng-fà/qióngfà	ADJ barren (land), waste(land)
廣	kuǎng/guǎng	ADJ °wide, vast VT expand
角	chüéh/jué	N horn, corner
羊角	yáng-chüéh/yángjué	N whirlwind
氣	ch'ì/qì	N breath, °air, vapour, ether; spiritual power, spirit
斥	ch'ìh/chì	N salt lands VT blame, scold; dismiss; extend, enlarge
鷃	yèn/yàn	N small bird like quail
斥鷃	ch'ìh-yèn/chìyàn	N quail
騰	t'éng/téng	VI jump, ascend VT mount
騰躍	t'éng-yüèh/téngyuè	VT °leap up, prance
翱	áo	VI soar like a bird
翔	hsíang/xíang	VI soar
翱翔	áo-hsíang/áoxíang	VI °flutter, soar
蒿	hāo	N wormwood, artemesia

莊子 逍遙遊 c.1

惠子謂莊子曰："魏王貽我大瓠之種，我樹之成，而實五石。以盛水漿，其堅不能自舉也。剖之以為瓢，則瓠落無所容。非不呺然大也，吾為其無用而掊之。"

莊子曰："夫子固拙於用大矣！宋人有善為不龜手之藥者，世世以洴澼絖為事。客聞之，請買其方百金。聚族而謀曰：'我世世為洴澼絖，不過數金；今一朝而鬻技百金，請與之。'客得之，以說吳王。越有難，吳王使之¹將，冬與越人水戰，大敗越人。裂地而封之。能不龜手，一也；或以封，或不免於洴澼絖，則所用之異也。今子有五石之瓠，何不慮以為大樽而浮乎江湖，而憂其瓠落無所容？則夫子猶有蓬之心也夫！"

---

1 之 refers to the man who bought the ointment.

Vocabulary

貽	í/yí	VT °give as a present, bequeath; leave behind
瓠	hù	N gourd
種	chǔng/zhǒng	N °seed; kind, sort
	chùng/zhòng	VT sow, plant
漿	chiāng/jiāng	N broth
剖	p'ŏu/pōu	VT split, divide
瓢	p'iáo/piáo	N gourd, °ladle
落	lò/luò	VI fall, drop, scatter N village
瓠落	hù-lò/hùluò	ADJ broad and shallow
呺	hsiāo/xiāo	ADJ vast and hollow
	háo	VT shout, cry
掊	p'ŏu/pǒu	VT °smash
	p'óu/póu	VT grasp with hands
拙	chō/zhuō	VT be clumsy, stupid
龜	chūn/jūn	ADJ chapped (also written 皸)
藥	yào	N °medicine, herbs, drugs
洴	p'íng/píng	VT bleach
澼	p'ì/pì	VT bleach
絖	k'uàng/kuàng	N floss-silk
買	mǎi	VT buy
吳	wú	N °name of one of the Chinese states; a surname VI speak in a loud voice
冬	tūng/dōng	N winter
裂	lièh/liè	VT tear apart, tear, °split
樽	tsūn/zūn	N sacrificial cup; goblet, wine-jar; °goblet shaped boat
湖	hú	N lake

莊子 胠篋 c.10

夫川竭而谷虛，丘夷而淵實。聖人已死，則大盜不起，天下平而無故矣。聖人不死，大盜不止。雖重[1]聖人而治天下，則是重利盜跖[2]也。為之斗斛以量之，則並與斗斛而竊之；為之權衡以稱之，則並與權衡而竊之；為之符璽以信之，則並與符璽而竊之；為之仁義以矯之，則並與仁義而竊之。何以知其然邪？彼竊鉤者誅，竊國者為諸侯。諸侯之門，而仁義存焉。則是非竊仁義聖知邪？故逐於大盜、揭諸侯、竊仁義並斗斛權衡符璽之利者，雖有軒冕[3]之賞弗能勸。斧鉞之威弗能禁。此重利盜跖而使不可禁者，是乃聖人之過也。故曰："魚不可脫於淵，國之利器不可以示人"。彼聖人者，天下之利器也，非所以明天下也。

故絕聖棄知，大盜乃止；擿玉毀珠，小盜不起；焚符破璽，而民朴鄙；掊斗折衡，而民不爭；殫殘天下之聖法，而民始可與論議。擢亂六律，鑠絕竽瑟，塞瞽曠[4]之耳，而天下始人含其聰矣；滅文章，散五采，膠離朱[5]之目，而天下始人含

1　重, to double.
2　盜跖, Robber Chih, a legendary figure of the Warring States period, said to have been the leader of a large band of brigands. He appears in the *Chuang-tzu* as the hero of a school of philosophy that derided all the Confucian virtues.
3　軒冕 refers to a high position with a good salary.
4　瞽曠 was a famous musician of the Spring and Autumn period, also known as 師曠.
5　離朱, Li Chu, also known as Li Lou 離婁, a legendary figure of ancient times who was able to see the tip of a hair from a distance of 100 paces.

其明矣；毀絕鉤繩，而棄規矩，攦工倕¹之指，而天下始人有其巧矣。故曰：大巧若拙。削曾史²之行，鉗楊墨³之口，攘棄仁義，而天下之德始玄同矣。彼人含其明，則天下不鑠矣；人含其聰，則天下不累矣；人含其知，則天下不惑矣；人含其德，則天下不僻矣。彼曾、史、楊、墨、師曠、工倕、離朱，皆外立其德，而以爚亂天下者也。法之所無用也。

---

1 工倕, Craftsman Ch'ui, a legendary carpenter from the times of Emperor Yao, said to have been able to draw a perfect circle and square without the aid of a compass or square.
2 曾史: Tseng Shen 曾參 and Shih Ch'iu 史鰌. Tseng Shen was renowned for his filial piety, and Shih Ch'iu as an upright official.
3 楊墨: Yang Chu 楊朱 and Mo Ti 墨翟, philosophers of the Warring States period. Yang Chu (c. 350 B.C.) was a representative of a school of philosophy which supported the nurturing of life. Mo Ti (late 5th century B.C.) was the founder of the Mohist school of philosophy. His best-known doctrine is universal love.

Vocabulary

胠	ch'ū/qū	VT °prise open, rifle N rib, arm-pit
篋	ch'iè/qiè	N small box
川	ch'uān/chuān	N °stream, flowing water
谷	kǔ/gǔ	N °valley, gorge; cereal, grain; millet
丘	ch'iū/qiū	N °hill, mound
跖	chíh/zhí	N °a proper name VT tread
斗	tǒu/dǒu	N °a measure for grain: peck; wine goblet; the Dipper
斛	hú	N a measure for grain: bushel
並	pìng/bìng	VT combine, merge ADV °equally; at the same time CONJ and
衡	héng	ADV horizontally N beam of a balance, °scales ADJ horizontal VI weigh
符	fú	N °a tally issued by a ruler to generals, envoys, etc., as a credential; symbol; magic figures drawn by Taoist priests to invoke or expel spirits and bring good or ill fortune; talisman VI tally with; accord with
璽	hsǐ/xǐ	N imperial or royal seal
鉤	kōu/gōu	N °buckle, hook; an ancient Chinese weapon; sickle VT hook ADJ bent
逐	chú/zhú	VT expel, °follow, pursue ADV one after the other, successively
軒	hsüān/xuān	ADJ high, lofty N °a high fronted carriage with curtains; small room with window; window or door
冕	miěn/miǎn	N crown; °ceremonial hat worn by officials
鉞	yüèh/yuè	N battle-axe
脫	t'ō/tuō	VT come off, take off; abandon; escape from; °get out of; neglect, slight
示	shìh/shì	N sign, omen VT °show, manifest
擿	chìh/zhì	VT scratch; °throw away (used for 擲)

焚	fén	VT °burn, set fire to
朴	p'ŭ/pŭ	ADJ simple, plain
鄙	pĭ/bĭ	N an out-of-the-way place; ward: local organization during Chou dynasty comprising 500 families; small town ADJ °simple, plain; mean, coarse VT look down on, despise
爭	chēng/zhēng	VT compete for, contend VI °struggle, wrangle N disturbance, quarrel
殫	tān/dān	VI use up, exhaust ADV °entirely, utterly
殘	ts'án/cán	VT °destroy, injure, damage ADJ incomplete; savage; cruel N cruelty; remnant
擢	chó/zhuó	VT °pull out, extract; raise, select for promotion
律	lǜ	N law, rule; °pitch-pipes VT restrain, keep under control
鑠	shuò	VT °melt; weaken ADJ brilliant, dazzling, lustrous (used for 爍)
竽	yǘ/yú	N an ancient wind instrument
瑟	sè	N twenty-five-stringed musical instrument
塞	sāi	VT °block, shut; fill up N stopper
	sài	N pass; place of strategic importance
瞽	kŭ/gŭ	ADJ blind
曠	k'uàng/kuàng	N °a proper name ADJ vast; free VT neglect
含	hán	VT hold something in the mouth; °contain, include; cherish, nurse
聰	ts'ūng/cōng	N faculty of hearing; acute hearing
滅	mièh/miè	VT extinguish, °destroy VI be extinguished
章	chāng/zhāng	N °ornament; pattern; chapter, stanza ADJ brilliant
采	ts'ăi/căi	N °bright colours VT gather
朱	chū/zhū	N bright red; °a surname ADJ red, cinnabar
矩	chǚ/jǚ	N °carpenter's square, rule, pattern

CHUANG-TZU c. 10

攦	lì	VT break
工	kūng/gōng	N work, craft; craftsman, °artisan ADJ skilful
倕	ch'uí/chuí	N a proper name
指	chǐh/zhǐ	N °finger VT point at; indicate
巧	ch'iǎo/qiǎo	ADJ skilful; clever, artful, cunning ADV opportunity N °skill
削	hsüēh/xuē	VT °pare, whittle, scrape; exterminate; cut off
曾	tsēng/zēng	N °a surname; relatives in two generations VT add (used for 增)
	ts'éng/céng	PART indicates perfective aspect: has/have... -ed
史	shǐh/shǐ	N history; °a surname
鉗	ch'ién/qián	VT °clamp; restrain N pincers, tongs
楊	yáng	N poplar; °a surname
墨	mò	N ink; °a surname ADJ black
攘	jǎng/rǎng	VT throw into confusion
	jáng/ráng	VT °reject, resist; seize, steal
玄	hsüán/xuán	ADJ black, °dark; abstruse; mysterious
惑	huò	N doubt VT mislead, °confuse
爚	yüèh/yuè	N blaze VT destroy, °dazzle

Kung-sun Lung Tzu 公孫龍子

THE *Kung-sun Lung Tzu* appears in the bibliographical section of the *Han-shu* 漢書 under the School of Names 名家. The philosophers of the School of Names, of which Kung-sun Lung is a representative, are variously called sophists, logicians or dialecticians. Kung-sun Lung said that his thought aimed to reconcile differences, affirm negatives and distinguish the particularity and generality of things. He was also a master of paradoxes, the most famous of which is "a white horse is not a horse".

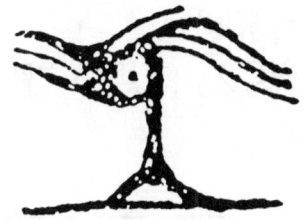

公孫龍子　白馬論

"白馬非馬可乎？"

曰："可。"

曰："何哉？"

曰："馬者所以命形也，白者所以命色也。命色者非命形也，故曰：白馬非馬。"

曰："有白馬，不可謂無馬也；不可謂無馬者，非馬也？有白馬為有馬，白之非馬，何也？"

曰："求馬，黃黑馬皆可致。求白馬，黃黑馬不可致。使白馬乃馬也，是所求一也；所求一者，白馬不異馬也。"

"所求不異，如黃黑馬，有可有不可，何也？"

"可與不可，其相非明，故黃黑馬，一也；而可以應'有馬'，而不可以應'有白馬'，是白馬之非馬，審矣。"

曰："以馬之有色為非馬，天下非有無色之馬也；天下無馬可乎？"

曰："馬固有色，故有白馬。使馬無色，有馬如[1]已耳。安取白馬？故白者，非馬也。白馬者，馬與白也，馬與白馬也。故曰：白馬非馬也。"

曰："馬未與白為馬，白未與馬為白。合馬與白，復名白馬，是相與。以不相與為名，未可。故曰：白馬非馬，未可。"

曰："以有白馬為有馬，謂有白馬為有黃馬，可乎？"

---

[1] For 如 some editions have 而.

曰:"未可。"

曰:"以有馬為異有黃馬,是異黃馬於馬也。異黃馬於馬,是以黃馬為非馬。以黃馬為非馬,而以白馬為有馬,此飛者入池,而棺槨異處,此天下之悖言亂辭也。"

曰:"有白馬不可謂無馬者,離白之謂也。是離者,有白馬不可謂有馬也。故所以為有馬者,獨以馬為有馬耳,非有白馬為有馬。故其為有馬也,不可以謂馬馬也。"

曰:"白者,不定所白,忘之而可也。白馬者,言白定所白也;定所白者,非白也。馬者,無去取於色,故黃黑皆所以應。白馬者,有去取於色,黃黑馬皆所以色去,故唯白馬獨可以應耳。無去者非有去也,故曰:白馬非馬。"

Vocabulary

孫	sūn	N grandchild, descendant
黑	hēi	ADJ °black, dark; secret N black
審	shěn	VT judge, examine ADJ °clear ADV carefully, in detail; clearly
棺	kuān/guān	N coffin, inner coffin
槨	kuǒ/guǒ	N outer coffin
悖	pèi/bèi	VI °be contrary to what is right; go against ADJ perverse; wrong N rebellion

Lun-yü 論語

THE *Lun-yü* (the *Analects*), the most famous of the Chinese Classics, is a record of the words and deeds of Confucius 孔子 (traditional dates 551-479 B.C.). His given name was Ch'iu 丘 and his style was Chung-ni 仲尼. Confucius himself denied that he had created a philosophy, calling himself a transmitter. However, he interpreted the pre-Confucian classics in terms of an ethical philosophy based on goodness. He gave traditional institutions ethical values.

The *Lun-yü* is a collection of short entries often in the form of dialogue between Confucius and his disciples. The book in its definitive form probably comes from late Chou or the beginning of Ch'in, and some scholars put it as late as the early Han dynasty. It is certain that it does not come from one hand, or even from one school. Some of the books have a decidedly Taoist orientation. The title was most probably coined at the beginning of the Han dynasty.

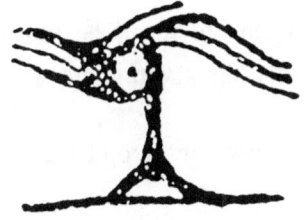

論語

II.3　子[1]曰："道[2]之以政，齊之以刑，民免而無恥；道之以德，齊之以禮，有恥且格。"

II.4　子曰："吾十有五而志于學，三十而立，四十而不惑，五十而知天命，六十而耳順，七十而從心所欲，不踰矩。"

II.20　季康子[3]問："使民敬忠以勸，如之何？"子曰："臨之以莊，則敬；孝慈，則忠；舉善而教不能，則勸。"

IV.5　子曰："富與貴，是人之所欲也；不以其道得之，不處也。貧與賤，是人之所惡也；不以其道得之，不去也。君子去仁，惡乎[4]成名？君子無終食之間[5]違仁，造次必於是，顛沛必於是。"

IV.8　子曰："朝聞道，夕可死矣。"

IV.14　子曰："不患無位，患所以立。不患莫己知，求為可知也。"

1　子, the Master, refers to Confucius.
2　道 is used for 導, to lead.
3　季康子 was a member of the Chi-sun 季孫 family, one of the three powerful families in the state of Lu 魯. His given name was Fei 肥, and K'ang was his posthumous name.
4　惡乎 = 惡於, where, how. Interrogative pronouns stand in front of prepositions.
5　終食之間, the time it takes to finish a meal, i.e., a short time.

VII.22　子曰："三人行，必有我師焉。擇其善者而從之，其不善者而改之。"

IX.13　子貢[6]曰："有美玉於斯，韞櫝而藏諸？求善賈而沽諸？"子曰："沽之哉！沽之哉！我待善賈者也。"

IX.14　子欲居九夷。或曰："陋，如之何？"子曰："君子居之，何陋之有？"

IX.17　子在川上，曰："逝者如斯夫！不舍晝夜。"

IX.23　子曰："後生可畏，焉知來者之不如今也？四十、五十而無聞焉，斯亦不足畏也已。"

IX.28　子曰："歲寒，然後知松柏之後彫也。"

XVIII.7　子路[7]從而後，遇丈人，以杖荷蓧。子路問曰："子見夫子乎？"丈人曰："四體不勤，五穀不分。孰為夫子？"植其杖而芸。子路拱而立。
　　止子路宿，殺雞為黍而食之，見其二子焉。
　　明日，子路行以告。
　　子曰："隱者也。"使子路反見之。至，則行矣。
　　子路曰："不仕無義。長幼之節，不可廢也；君臣之義，如之何其廢之？欲潔其身，而亂大倫。君子之仕也，行其義也。道之不行，已知矣。"

6　子貢 was one of the disciples of Confucius.
7　子路 was one of the disciples of Confucius.

Vocabulary

季	chì/jì	N °a surname; quarter of year, season; end of season or dynasty ADJ last in a series (e.g., youngest brother, last month of season)
康	k'āng/kāng	N °a proper name; ease, peace
敬	chìng/jìng	VI °be respectful, reverent
慈	tz'ú/cí	VI be kind (e.g., of parental feelings)
次	tz'ù/cì	VT arrange in order N place in a sequence, the next ADJ inferior
造次	tsào-tz'ù/zàocì	VI be hurried, °harassed
顛	tiēn/diān	VI fall down N top of head
沛	p'èi/pèi	ADJ abundant, great, torrential; copious VI hurry
顛沛	tiēn-p'èi/diānpèi	VI fall prostrate
夕	hsī/xī	N °evening, night
改	kǎi/gǎi	VT change, °correct
貢	kùng/gòng	N °proper name; tribute; revenue VT offer as tribute
韞	yǔn/yùn	VT °wrap, store
櫝	tú/dú	N wooden box VT °put in box
沽	kū/gū	VT °sell, buy
陋	lòu	ADJ °lowly, irregular, imperfect, poor
逝	shìh/shì	VI °pass by, go; die
晝	chòu/zhòu	N daytime
松	sūng/sōng	N pine tree
柏	pó/bó	N cypress (also pronounced pǎi/bǎi)
彫	tiāo/diāo	VI lose leaves, °wither (used for 凋) VT engrave, carve
丈	chàng/zhàng	N senior, °elder; a measure of 10 feet
杖	chàng/zhàng	N staff, °stick VT beat
荷	hò/hè	VT °carry
	hó/hé	N lotus

篠	tiào/diào	N bamboo basket
勤	ch'ín/qín	VI toil VT aid ADJ °diligent
植	chíh/zhí	VT °plant, set up
芸	yǔn/yún	N rue (a strong scented herb), the yellow colour of withered flowers VI °weed
拱	kǔng/gǒng	VT °clasp hands in front of breast (a sign of respect); surround, span with hands, hold
黍	shǔ	N °millet, grain
仕	shìh/shì	VI take office
潔	chiéh/jié	VT °make or cause to be pure ADJ clean, pure, clear

Lao-tzu 老子

THE *Lao-tzu* is also known as the *Tao-te-ching* 道德經. Traditionally it is said to be the work of Lao-tzu who, again according to tradition, was an older contemporary of Confucius. His surname is given as Li 李, and his given name either Tan 聃 or Erh 耳. There are a number of stories in which Confucius asks Lao-tzu for advice and instruction; all are legendary in nature. Current thinking places the work in the third century B.C. The teaching of the *Lao-tzu* is based on a Way or *Tao*, an ineffable reality which is eternal, spontaneous, the source of all things and the way followed by all things.

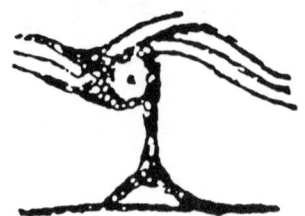

老子 c.2

天下皆知美之為美，斯惡已；皆知善之為善，斯不善已。故有無¹相生，難易相成，長短相形，高下相傾，音聲相和，前後相隨。是以聖人處無為之事，行不言之教。萬物作焉而不辭²，生而不有，為而不恃，功成而弗居。夫唯弗居，是以不去。

老子 c.80

小國寡民，使有什伯³之器而不用，使民重死而不遠徙。雖有舟輿，無所乘之；雖有甲兵，無所陳之。使人復結繩⁴而用之，甘其食，美其服，安其居，樂其俗。鄰國相望，雞犬之聲相聞，民至老死不相往來。

---

1 有無, being and non-being.
2 辭, to interfere.
3 什伯, tenfold and one-hundredfold, i.e., many.
4 結繩, to tie knots in a rope; a method of recording events before the advent of writing.

LAO-TZU

Vocabulary

傾	chīng/qīng	VI incline, °lean on; collapse N deviation VT empty
恃	shìh/shì	VI °rely on; depend on
什	shíh/shí	N a unit or group of ten (e.g. soldiers, households)
結	chiéh/jié	VT °tie; knit; knot; weave; form; settle
	chiēh/jiē	VT bear (fruit)
甘	kān/gān	ADJ sweet, pleasant, willing ADV willingly VT °enjoy

Tso-chuan 左傳

THE *Tso-chuan* is a "commentary" on the *Spring and Autumn Annals* 春秋, a very terse chronological account of the state of Lu 魯 covering the so-called Spring and Autumn period, i.e., 722-481 B.C. The *Tso-chuan* covers a longer period than the *Spring and Autumn Annals*, viz. 722-463 B.C. and gives much more information about the period as well as information about the other states. According to tradition it was written by Tso Ch'iu-ming 左丘明, a contemporary of Confucius. Some scholars place it between 468 and 300 B.C., some as late as the Han dynasty.

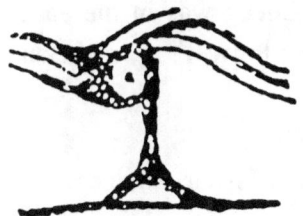

左傳・僖公三十年[1]

晉侯、秦伯[2]圍鄭，以其無禮于晉，且貳于楚也。晉軍函陵[3]，秦軍氾南[4]。

佚之狐[5]言于鄭伯[6]曰："國危矣，若使燭之武[7]見秦君，師必退。"公從之。辭曰："臣之壯也，猶不如人；今老矣，無能為也已。"公曰："吾不能早用子，今急而求子，是寡人之過也。然鄭亡，子亦有不利焉。"許之。

夜縋而出，見秦伯，曰："秦、晉圍鄭，鄭既知亡矣。若亡鄭而有益於君，敢以煩執事[8]。越國以鄙遠[9]，君知其難也。焉用亡鄭以陪鄰？鄰之厚，君之薄也。若舍鄭以為東道主，行李之往來，共[10]其乏困，君亦無所害。且君嘗為晉君賜[11]矣，許君焦、瑕，朝濟而夕設版[12]焉，君之

---

1 The thirtieth year of Duke Hsi is 630 B.C.
2 晉侯、秦伯: 晉文公 (697-627 B.C.) and 秦穆公 (?-621 B.C.).
3 函陵, a place outside the border of Cheng 鄭.
4 氾南, a place south of the River Fan outside the border of Cheng.
5 佚之狐, I Chih-hu, an official of the state of Cheng.
6 鄭伯 is 鄭文公.
7 燭之武, Chu Chih-wu, a Grand Master 大夫 of Cheng.
8 執事, refers to officials who have been assigned special responsibility by the ruler; here, however, the term seems to refer to the Duke of Ch'in.
9 越國, to cross a state. Cheng was in the east, Ch'in in the west, and Chin between the two. 鄙, a border town. 鄙遠, make an out-of-the-way place a border town.
10 共 used for 供, to supply.
11 賜 here means to bestow a favour, kindness.
12 設版, to build defences.

所知也。夫晉,何厭之有?既東封鄭,又欲肆其西封。若不闕秦,將焉取之?闕秦以利晉,唯君圖之。"秦伯説,與鄭人盟。使杞子、逢孫、楊孫[1]戍之,乃還。

子犯[2]請擊之。公[3]曰:"不可!微[4]夫人之力不及此。因人之力而敝之,不仁;失其所與[5],不知;以亂易整,不武。吾其還也。"亦去之。

---

1 杞子、逢孫、楊孫, Ch'i-tzu, P'ang-sun and Yang-sun were all officials in the state of Ch'in 秦.
2 子犯 Tzu-fan, the style of 狐偃, Hu Yen, a Grand Master of Chin.
3 Duke Wen of Chin.
4 微 is used like 非, if it were not for.
5 與, to make an alliance.

Vocabulary

僖	hsī/xī	N a proper name; amusement
圍	wéi	VT enclose, °surround ADV all round
貳	èrh/èr	NUM two N deputy ADV once again VI °be double-minded ADJ different; irregular
函	hán	N °a place name; armour; case or cover for books; letter VT contain, envelop
陵	líng	N °mound VT ride; cross, traverse; insult
氾	fàn	VT overflowing, inundate N °a place name
佚	ì/yì	N °a surname ADJ idleness, ease VI err; lose
燭	chú/zhú	N a proper name; candle VT illumine
早	tsǎo/zǎo	ADJ & ADV early, in the morning; former(ly), °previous(ly)
急	chí/jí	VI feel anxious; hurried VT °feel anxious or impatient about something; treat as urgent ADV hurriedly
縋	chuì/zhuì	VT let down with a rope
益	ì/yì	N °benefit, advantage ADJ beneficial VT increase ADV increasingly
煩	fán	VI be irritated, be annoyed; be tired of VT disturb; °trouble
執	chíh/zhí	VT grasp, hold; °manage, direct
執事	chíh-shìh/zhíshì	N work, job; °person in charge of specified duties
陪	p'éi/péi	VT °add; accompany; assist; indemnify, reimburse (used for 賠)
李	lǐ	N plum; surname; °envoy
行李	hsíng-lǐ/xínglǐ	N luggage; envoy

困	k'ùn/kùn	N distress; poverty; °weariness VI be surrounded; be in straitened circumstances, impoverished
焦	chiāo/jiāo	ADJ burnt; anxious N coke; surname; °name of a city in Cheng
瑕	hsiá/xiá	N flaw; defeat; °name of a city in Cheng
濟	chì/jì	VT °cross a river; aid, help; benefit; stop N success
設	shè	VT establish, °set up, arrange CONJ if
版	pǎn/bǎn	N °board, wall; printing plate
厭	yèn/yàn	VT dislike; be bored by; be satiated by VI °be satisfied; be satiated
肆	ssù/sì	VT indulge, °extend, develop; show, display ADJ apparent; extreme N shop, market
闕	ch'üèh/què	N watchtower on either side of a palace or city gate; imperial palace
	ch'üēh/quē	N fault, error (used for 缺) VT °destroy, debilitate ADJ incomplete; imperfect
盟	méng	N alliance; sworn (brothers) VT °form an alliance
杞	ch'ǐ/qǐ	N medlar tree; °a proper name
戍	shù	VT defend, °guard frontiers
犯	fàn	VT transgress, offend N criminal; °a proper name
敝	pì/bì	ADJ shabby, worn-out VT get rid of, destroy, °defeat PRON my, this
整	chěng/zhěng	VT arrange, put in order ADJ °orderly; whole

左傳・莊公十年[1]

十年春，齊師伐我[2]。公[3]將戰。曹劌[4]請見。其鄉人[5]曰："肉食者[6]謀之，又何間[7]焉？"劌曰："肉食者鄙，未能遠謀。"乃入見。問："何以戰？"公曰："衣食所安，弗敢專也，必以分人。"對曰："小惠未遍，民弗從也。"公曰："犧牲玉帛，弗敢加[8]也，必以信。"對曰："小信未孚，神弗福也。"公曰："小大之獄，雖不能察，必以情。"對曰："忠之屬也。可以一戰。戰則請從。"公與之乘。戰於長勺[9]。

公將鼓之。劌曰："未可。"齊人三鼓。劌曰："可矣。"齊師敗績。公將馳之。劌曰："未可。"下視其轍，登軾而望之，曰："可矣。"遂逐齊師。

既克，公問其故。對曰："夫戰，勇氣也。一鼓作氣，再而衰，三而竭。彼竭我盈，故克之。夫大國難測也，懼有伏焉。吾視其轍亂，望其旗靡，故逐之。"

---

1 The tenth year of Duke Chuang is 684 B.C.
2 In the previous year, Lu 魯 and Ch'i 齊 signed a treaty which had now been broken by Ch'i. 我 refers to "our state", i.e., Lu.
3 Duke Chuang of Lu 魯莊公.
4 曹劌, Ts'ao Kuei, a brave warrior in the service of Duke Chuang.
5 鄉人, person from the same native place.
6 肉食者, the meat-eaters, refers to those in high positions with high salaries.
7 間, to come between, to intervene.
8 加, to add to, here meaning to add to or go beyond the traditional rules for sacrifice.
9 長勺 Ch'ang-shao, a place in Lu.

Vocabulary

曹	ts'áo/cáo	N °a surname; official, staff; suffix indicating the plural
劌	kuèi/guì	VT cut, wound N °a proper name
犧	hsī/xī	N sacrifice; animal of a uniform colour used in sacrifices
牲	shēng	N domestic animal; sacrificial animal
犧牲	hsī-shēng/xīshēng	N °sacrificial animal
孚	fú	N trustworthiness VT °inspire confidence VI float on the surface (used for 浮)
獄	yù/yù	N prison; lawsuit, °trial
勺	sháo	N ladle, spoon
績	chī/jī	N achievement, merit VI spin thread
敗績	paì-chī/baìjī	VT be defeated
馳	ch'íh/chí	VI speed, gallop; move eagerly towards VT °pursue
轍	ché/zhé	N °wheel track; rhyme (of a song or a poem)
軾	shìh/shì	N crossbar used as an armrest at the front of a carriage
克	k'ò/kè	AUX V be able to VT °overcome, subdue; control
勇	yǔng/yǒng	N valour ADJ °brave
衰	shuāi	VI °decline, wane
	ts'uī/cuī	VI decrease progressively N mourning garment
盈	yíng	VI °be full of; be filled with VT have a surplus of; fill ADJ full
測	ts'è/cè	VT measure, °estimate, fathom; conjecture
伏	fú	VI prostrate oneself, submit; °lie in ambush
旗	ch'í/qí	N °flag, banner
靡	mǐ	VI blown away by the wind; °fall ADJ extravagant; gorgeous NEG ADV no, not
	mí	VT disperse

Grammatical Notes

THE grammatical notes offered here are not meant to be exhaustive; they are meant to cover only the most important aspects of Classical Chinese grammar. The notes are divided into three main sections: The Sentence, Content Words and Function Words. The sections at times overlap, in particular the first with the third. It was, however, felt that the repetition of points already made in the section dealing with the sentence under the relevant function word would be useful. The examples chosen to illustrate the grammatical points have been taken as far as possible from the texts included in this book; page and line numbers are given after the English translation.

Classical Chinese, like Modern Chinese, is an uninflected language, that is, words do not change according to gender, number, tense, case, aspect, etc. In such a language the position of words in the sentence and words with a grammatical function are of primary importance. For this reason it is important to remember that the qualifier comes before the word it qualifies, i.e., an adjective will stand before the noun it qualifies, the adverb before the verb or adjective it qualifies, etc. There are a few exceptions to this rule which will be discussed below (p. 149). It is equally important to remember that a word that generally functions as, for example, a noun may function as a verb if it is used in the position of a verb; this, too, will be discussed below (pp. 152, 155, 156).

There are two categories of words in Classical Chinese, called full words 實詞 and empty words 虛詞 in Chinese; full words are content words, such as nouns, verbs, adjectives, and empty words are function words or particles, that is, words with a grammatical function.

The Sentence

The sentence in Classical Chinese, just as in Modern Chinese, follows a simple word order—subject and predicate. The subject is a noun or a nominal clause and the predicate consists of a verb and other elements such as an indirect object, an object and a complement. The predicate may also be a nominal clause. The topic for discussion, which is not necessarily the grammatical subject of the sentence, is often placed in an exposed position at the beginning of the sentence and in such cases it is more precise to speak of topics for discussion or topical subjects and predicates. Topical subjects may be used to introduce a topic, to give emphasis or contrast, or to avoid awkwardness in style. This will be discussed more fully below (p. 149).

The common patterns of simple sentences are:

S	P			
	V	IO	OBJ	Complement
其良人 The husband	出。 went out. (2.1)			
孟子 Mencius	見 saw		梁惠王。 King Hui of Liang. (10.1)	
楚王 The King of Ch'u	賜 gave	晏子 Yen-tzu	酒。 wine. (71.6)	
伯牙 Po-ya	游 went on an excursion			於泰山之陰。 to the south side of Mt T'ai. (74.4)
和氏 Mr Ho	得 found		玉璞 a piece of unpolished jade	[於]楚山中。 [on] the Ch'u mountain. (52.1)
吾 I	將曳 shall drag		尾 [my] tail	於塗中。 in the mud. (102b.6)

GRAMMATICAL NOTES

The Sentence with a Nominal Predicate

I   The sentence with a nominal predicate (or equational sentence) is one in which both the subject and the predicate are nominal, without a linking verb, e.g.:

是亦走也。	This too is running away. (13.8)
吾邱吾子也。	I am Ch'iu-wu-tzu. (64.6)
南冥者，天池也。	The southern sea is the heavenly pool. (109.4)

Note that in the first example 是 is a demonstrative pronoun and that 是 is rarely used as the verb "to be" in Classical Chinese. It starts to appear as a verb in the Han dynasty. The pattern for equational sentences is: A (者) B (者)也 and can be translated "A is B". The function of 也 and often of 者 is to stress the preceding construction, but they are not essential: A B and A 者 B, also occasionally occur.

II   Adverbs such as 乃 or 即 (in fact, precisely) may be used to stress an equational sentence, e.g.:

是乃仁術也。	This was in fact an artifice of goodness. (27.11)

Other words of emphasis such as 必 and 誠 may also be used:

是誠不能也。	This is really to be incapable. (28.7)
千乘之國，弒其君者，必百乘之家。	The one who kills the ruler of a state of a thousand war chariots will certainly be from a family of a hundred war chariots. (10.7)

III   The negative adverb used in equational sentences is 非: A 非 B 也, A is not B, for example:

故王之不王，不為也，非不能也。	Therefore a king's not being a king is a case of not doing; it is not a case of being incapable. (28.4)
子非魚。	You are not a fish. (104b.3)
子非我。	You are not me. (104b.4)

IV   The closest to a copula verb in Classical Chinese is 為; however, it is not used very often and, when it is, the final 也 is omitted. The difference between the two is that the equational sentence without a verb implies a timeless truth, while the sentence using 為 does not. 為 may also be used in sentences that require auxiliary verbs or aspect particles that cannot be used in sentences with a nominal predicate.

是方四十里為阱於國中。	This forty *li* square is a trap in the middle of the kingdom. (35.10)
然後可以為民父母。	Afterwards, one may be a parent to the people. (39.13)
斯足為戒矣。	This is sufficient to be a warning. (64.16)
輿薪之不見，為不用明焉。	That a cartload of firewood is not seen, is [because of] not using one's sight for it. (28.2)
孟嘗君為相數十年…	Lord Meng-ch'ang was Prime Minister for several tens of years... (83.24)

V   Questions asking "what" or "why" are often put in the form of an equational sentence. The pattern is A 何也, A is why/what?, i.e., why or what is A?

寡人之囿方四十里，民猶以為大，何也？	My park is 40 *li* square, yet the people still consider it large—why? (35.5)

VI   Finally, equational sentences are often used to express a cause or reason for something:

妾之美我者，畏我也。	My concubine considers me handsome because she stands in awe of me. (78.10)

The Interrogative Sentence

I   Interrogative particles are placed at the end of affirmative sentences when an affirmative or negative response is sought. Commonly used particles are:

乎	a general final interrogative particle similar to the modern 嗎 or 呢.
諸	a fusion of 之 + 乎 used at the end of a sentence.
歟、與、邪	final interrogative particles often used in rhetorical questions, in questions asking for a choice to be made, or after nominal predicates.

Some examples:

齊桓、晉文之事可得聞乎？	May I hear of the affairs of Huan of Ch'i and Wen of Chin? (26.1)
若是其大乎？	Was it so big? (35.3)
不識有諸？	I do not know whether it was so. (26.13)
然則廢釁鐘與？	So then, are we to give up consecrating the bell? (implies "surely not") (26.12)

GRAMMATICAL NOTES

天之蒼蒼，其正色邪，其遠而無所至極邪？	The azure of the sky, is it its true colour, or is it [because of] its distance and limitlessness? (109.7)
今子欲以子之梁國而嚇我邪？	Now do you want, because of your state of Liang, to shoo me away? (implies "you do") (104a.6)
今恩足以及禽獸，而功不至於百姓者，獨何與？	Now [your] graciousness is sufficient to reach to the animals but the benefit does not reach the people, however can it be? (28.1)

亦⋯乎 and 不亦⋯乎 are used in rhetorical questions:

亦將有以利吾國乎？	Surely you will have the means to profit my kingdom? (10.2)
民以為小，不亦宜乎？	Is it not right that the people should consider it small? (35.7)
不亦悲乎？	Is it not sad? (110.1)

II In questions asking for information about some element in the sentence, interrogative pronouns, adjectives or adverbs are used:

何	Pronoun used when asking questions about things: what, why. Adverb: why, how. Adjective: what, what kind.
曷	Pronoun: what. Adverb: why, how.
誰	Pronoun used when asking questions about people: who.
孰	Pronoun used when asking questions about people or things: who, which, which one; often used in comparisons.
安	Pronoun: where, what. Adverb: how, where.
惡	Pronoun: what, where. Adverb: how, where.
奚	Pronoun: which. Adjective: what, where. Adverb: why, how, which one.
胡	Adverb: why, how.
盍	Adverb: why not.
焉	Pronoun: how, where.

GRAMMATICAL NOTES

豈 — Adverb used in rhetorical questions. If the question is in the affirmative form, the implied answer is negative; if it is in the negative form, the implied answer is positive. It is frequently used with a final 哉 or 乎.

Some examples:

何以利吾國？	How can you profit my kingdom? (10.4)
王，何必曰利？	Your Majesty, why must you speak of profit? (10.3)
鄰國之民不加少，寡人之民不加多，何也？	Why is it that the people of neighbouring states do not decrease and my people do not increase? (13.4)
孟嘗君曰："客何好？"	Lord Meng-ch'ang said: "What does the guest like?" (81.2)
子奚哭之悲也？	Why do you weep so grievously? (52.8)
其一能鳴，其一不能鳴，請奚殺？	One of them is able to cackle, the other is unable; may I ask which one should I kill? (99.5)
此誰也？	Who is this? (82.1)
我孰與城北徐公美？	Who is more handsome, I or Mr Hsü from the north of the city? (78.2)
子非魚。安知魚之樂？	You are not a fish, how do you know the happiness of a fish? (104b.3)
彼惡知之？	How should they know it? (27.7)
是豈水之性哉？	How can this be the nature of water? (implies: surely it cannot be). (44.7)

When interrogative pronouns are used as subjects the word order is the same as in the affirmative sentence. However, when they are used as objects they precede the verb or preposition. For examples see section on changes in word order (p. 149).

III   A number of idiomatic phrases are used to ask questions such as: like what? what is to be done? what would one think or say? how does one deal with? They are 如何, 若何 and 奈何. A noun or the pronoun object 之 may be placed between the two characters to form the following phrases: 如之何, 如⋯何, 若之何, 若⋯何, 奈之何, 奈⋯何.

如之何則可？	What can I do about it to make it possible/right? (22.4)

GRAMMATICAL NOTES

四境之內不治，則如之何？	If the country is not well governed, what is to be done? (37.7)
市義奈何？	What is the use of buying righteousness? (82.21)

何如 is used with the same meaning as 如何. The change in the order of the two words was possibly introduced to conform with the rule that an interrogative pronoun stands before the preposition or verb of which it is an object.

Some examples:

以五十步笑百步，則何如？	If because of their fifty paces they laughed at the one hundred paces, what would you say/think? (13.7)
以子之矛，陷子之楯，何如？	If one pierced your shield with your spear, how about it/what would happen? (55a.3)

The Conditional Sentence

I At times context alone gives the sentence a conditional meaning, e.g.:

見其生，不忍見其死。	If he sees them alive, he cannot bear to see them dead. (27.12)
二者不可得兼，舍魚而取熊掌者也。	If the two cannot be obtained at the same time, I shall give up the fish and take the bear's paw. (46.2)

Conditional sentences may also be formed by juxtaposing two simple predicates: 不奪不饜, If they do not snatch, they are not satisfied (10.9). This construction is often used to indicate a universal truth. The conditional relationship is implied by the context.

II The particles 若 or 如 may be placed at the beginning of the sentence or after the subject; it may also be used together with 則 at the beginning of the second clause:

王如知此，則無望民之多於鄰國也。	If Your Majesty knows this, do not expect that your people will be more numerous than those in neighbouring states. (14.1)
王如施仁政於民…	If Your Majesty extends a benevolent government to the people… (22.5)

Or 則 may be used on its own at the beginning of the second clause; 斯 is also used in this way.

今君人者，釋其刑德而使臣用之，則君反制於臣矣。	Now if the ruler discards his punishment and reward and allows the ministers to use them, the ruler will instead be ruled by the ministers. (61.11)
彼人含其明，則天下不鑠矣。	If men contain their eyesight, there will be no dazzle in the world. (117.4)
王無罪歲，斯天下之民至焉。	If Your Majesty does not blame the harvest, the people of the world will come to you. (15.3)

III The word 苟 is also used to introduce "if" clauses (in this example 苟為 is an idiomatic expression with the same meaning as 苟):

苟為後義而先利…	If you place righteousness last and profit first... (10.8)

Aspect

A number of particles are used to show the future or past aspect of the verb; some are final particles and some stand in front of the verb.

I 矣 is a final particle used after verbal predicates to indicate completion of the action of the verb or that a new situation has arisen. It is similar to the modern 了.

王無親臣矣。	Your Majesty has no close ministers. (39.2)
斯有不忍人之政矣。	Thus they had policies which were sympathetic to the people. (49.2)
五畝之宅，樹之以桑，五十者可以衣帛矣。	Plant a homestead of five *mu* with mulberries, so those who are fifty years old may wear silk. (14.7)
天下之刖者多矣。	There are many in the world who have had their feet cut off. (52.8)

The time reference may be past, present or future:

死已三千歲矣。	It has already been dead for three thousand years. (102b.3)
此哭哀則哀矣。	The grief of this weeping is grief indeed. (64.2)
上下交征利而國危矣。	If superiors and inferiors join in contending for profit the state will be in danger. (10.5)

II 既 is used in an adverbial position to show that the action of the verb has been completed. It is often used with 矣 to show that a new situation has arisen. It

GRAMMATICAL NOTES

can also occur together with 已, which is also used to show completed action (see III below).

兵刃既接…	The weapons and swords have joined… (13.6)
既克，公問其故。	After they had won the victory, the Duke asked the reason. (138.13)
既已知吾知之而問我。	Already knowing that I knew it, you asked me. (104b.8)
鄭既知亡矣。	Cheng knew it must perish. (134.8)

III 已 means "already" and is also used to show completion of action:

已得履，乃曰…	After he had found the shoes, he said… (55b.2)
聖人已死…	When the sages have died… (116.1)

IV 未 is a negative adverb which shows that the action of the verb has not yet or never been completed. In a subordinate clause at the beginning of the sentence it may be translated "before".

良人未之知也。	The husband did not yet know it. (3.6)
未有仁而遺其親者也。	There has never been one who was good yet neglected his parents. (10.9)
臣未之聞也。	I have never heard of it. (26.3)
見牛未見羊也。	You saw the ox but had never seen the sheep. (27.11)
未至百里，民扶老攜幼，迎君道中。	Before he was within a hundred *li*, the people supporting the old and leading the young, welcomed the lord on the road. (83.5)

V 嘗 and 曾 are used in an adverbial position to indicate the past tense:

吾負之，未嘗見也。	I have neglected him, I have never granted him an audience. (82.3)
臣則嘗能斲之。	I used to be able to slice it off. (102a.5)
三年之後，未嘗見全牛也。	After three years, I never saw the whole ox. (106.6)

VI 將 used in an adverbial position indicates the future tense. The meaning often implies that the subject intends to do something.

吾將瞷良人之所之也。	I shall (intend to) spy on our husband to see where he goes. (2.5)
將以釁鐘。	We intend to consecrate a bell with it. (26.11)

我將去之。	I am going to leave it. (41.7)
今人乍見孺子將入於井⋯	Now, if someone suddenly saw a child about to fall into a well... (49.4)
晏子將使楚。	Yen-tzu was going on a mission to Ch'u. (71.1)
吾將曳尾於塗中。	I shall drag my tail in the mud. (102b.6)

VII 且 is similar in meaning to 將.

鄭人有且置履者。	A man of Cheng was going to buy a pair of shoes. (55b.1)

Topic

The topic may be described as the logical subject of the sentence which is not the grammatical subject of the verb; generally it is the grammatical object that has been placed at the beginning of the sentence to give it prominence as the main topic of discussion, or for emphasis. The basic pattern is Topic + P, e.g.: 五畝之宅，樹之以桑, A homestead of five *mu*, plant it with mulberries (14.7), which in the ordinary word order would read 樹五畝之宅以桑. In this sentence the topic is resumed by 之 after the verb. Another example is:

青，取之於藍。	Blue comes from indigo (blue, take it from indigo). (92.1)

In some sentences the 之 is placed before the verb for even greater emphasis:

夫子之謂也。	Master [this] refers to you. (27.14)
殺戮之謂刑。	Public execution, it is called punishment. (61.2)

Changes to the Normal Word Order

I In sentences that contain negative adverbs such as 未, 莫 a pronoun object will commonly stand between the negative adverb and the verb, e.g., the negative form of 有之 is 未之有. However, the normal word order also sometimes occurs. Some examples are:

臣未之聞也。	I have never heard of it. (26.3)
然而不王者，未之有。	Such a situation has never occurred without one who acts as a true king. (14.11)
莫之能禦也。	No-one is able to withstand it. (26.5)

GRAMMATICAL NOTES

II   Interrogative pronoun objects generally stand before the verb or preposition, e.g., 安之, to go where; 安在, to be where; 何以, by what means, i.e., how; 何謂, to mean what; 何之, to go where. Some examples are:

何以利吾國？	How can I profit my kingdom? (10.4)
其一能鳴，其一不能鳴，請奚殺？	One of them is able to cackle, the other is unable; may I ask which one should I kill? (99.5)
吾欲辱之，何以也？	I want to humiliate him: how should I do it? (71.2)
客何好？	What does the guest like? (81.2)

III   In some cases a demonstrative pronoun object stands before its preposition. A common occurrence of this is 是以, for this reason, therefore. However, 以是 also occurs.

IV   The order of subject and predicate may be changed in emphatic sentences, e.g.:

善哉！子之聽夫！	Excellent indeed is your listening! (How well you listen!) (74.7)
賢哉回也！	Worthy indeed was Hui!

V   Adverbs of degree are often placed after the word they modify as a separate predicate:

君美甚。	You are the acme of beauty. (lit., You are beautiful, extremely.) (78.3)
王之蔽甚矣！	The deception of Your Majesty is extreme! (78.16)

VI   Numbers stand directly in front of the noun they modify, they are, however, sometimes placed after the noun in the following ways:

(a)   Placed after the noun in apposition:

吏二縛一人詣王。	Two officials bound a man and went up to the king. (71.6)
孟嘗君予車五十乘。	Lord Meng-ch'ang gave him 50 carriages. (83.10)
地方百里而可以王。	One can rule a territory of 100 *li* square. (22.5)

(b)   Placed after a noun as a separate predicate:

文王之囿方七十里。	The park of King Wen was 70 *li* square. (35.6)

Ellipsis

When the meaning is clear from the context, subjects, objects and prepositions are generally omitted. For example, once a subject is introduced it need not be repeated until there is a change of subject; the same is true of the object.

I   Omitted subject:

The simplest example is in dialogue where the speaker is identified only the first time he/she speaks: 王曰…。孟子曰…。曰…。曰…。   Other examples:

蚤起，施從良人之所之。	Rising early [she, i.e., the wife] followed her husband along a winding path. (3.1)
卒之東郭墦閒。	Finally [he, i.e., the husband] went to the graveyard on the eastern outskirts. (3.2)
則凍餒其妻子。	Then [he] found that his wife and children had been cold and hungry. (37.2)
奉而獻之厲王。	[He] respectfully offered it to King Li. (52.1)
今方來。	Now [he] has just come. (71.2)
於是入朝見威王。	Thereupon [he] went to court to see King Wei. (78.12)

II   Omitted object:

皆以美于徐公。	They all thought [me] more handsome than Mr Hsü. (78.14)
使王天下。	Made [him] rule the empire. (57.3)
與坐談。	Sat and talked with [him]. (78.6)

III   Omitted verb:

子曰：…擇其善者而從之，其不善而改之。	The Master said:... I shall choose his good points to imitate them, and [choose] his bad points to correct myself. (127.1)

IV   Omitted preposition:

楚人和氏得玉璞楚山中。	Mr Ho, a native of Ch'u, found a piece of unpolished jade [on] the Ch'u mountain. (52.1)

GRAMMATICAL NOTES

Content Words

Nouns

Nouns and noun clauses serve as subjects, objects, qualifiers and nominal predicates.

Changes in Word Class:

I   Nouns used as verbs

A noun used as a verb may indicate:

(a)   the action performed by whatever the noun refers to:

兵之	to weapon him, i.e., to use a weapon to kill him
鼓之	to drum them, i.e., to use a drum to arouse them to action (13.5)

This rule does not always apply, e.g., 鼓琴 means "to play the zither", and 乃援琴而鼓之 means "He then took his zither and played it." (74.5)

(b)   a way of regarding someone or something:

師之	to treat or consider him as teacher
孟嘗君客我。	Lord Meng-ch'ang considers me (treats me as) a retainer. (81.11)

(c)   the behaviour the noun implies:

君不君。	The ruler does not behave as a ruler ought to behave.

(d)   movement in a certain direction:

奚以之九萬里而南為！	What use is it to rise to 90,000 *li* to go south? (109.15)

II   Nouns used as adverbs

When a noun is used as an adverb it implies similarity, manner or attitude:

今君有區區之薛，不拊愛子其民，因而賈利之。	Now you possess the small state of Hsüeh, but you do not cherish, love and treat its people like sons; consequently you profit from them like a merchant. (82.22)

A noun may also be used as an adverb indicating place:

山居而谷汲者。	Those who live on mountains draw their water in valleys.
塗有餓莩。	On the roads there are people who have died of starvation. (15.1)

or indicating time:

明日，徐公來。	The next day Mr Hsü came. (78.8)
朝聞道，夕死可矣。	If one hears the Way in the morning, it is possible to die in the evening. (126.13)

In front of a verb 日, 月 and 歲 often mean every day, every month and every year:

君子博學而日參省乎己。	A gentleman, in broadening his knowledge, daily examines himself. (92.4)

Pronouns

There are no specific plural forms for pronouns and no possessive forms for the first and second person pronouns. The plural sense is usually clear from the context; there are, however, a few nouns which indicate a group and which may be used with a pronoun to indicate the plural. One example is 輩. Also the adjective 諸 and the adverb 皆 may be used. The following are commonly used pronouns:

I   First person: 我，吾，予，余.
The pronoun 吾 is seldom used as an object; one exception is when it is the object between a negative adverb and verb (see p. 149), e.g., 莫吾知, no-one knows me. It was customary for people to refer to themselves by their given names 名, or by a humble form such as: 臣 used by a subject when addressing a ruler; 妾 used by a woman in addressing her husband or any man of her own or higher social status; 寡人 used by a ruler.

II   Second person: 女，汝，爾，若，乃，而.
The second person was used between equals or when addressing inferiors. Generally people were addressed by titles, such as 大王 to address a ruler; or honorific terms, such as 子, 君, 公.

III   Third person: 彼 is used occasionally, but it is really a demonstrative pronoun; others were usually referred to by their names or titles. 其 is the third person possessive and 之 the third person object.

GRAMMATICAL NOTES

IV   Reflexive personal pronouns:

己 "self" may be used as a pronoun in all positions:

虎不知獸畏己。	The tiger did not know the animals feared him. (89.7)

自 "oneself" always occurs immediately in front of the verb, and so is classed as an adverb. Used with a transitive verb without an object, it indicates that the subject and object are the same. Used with an intransitive verb or a transitive verb with an object, it shows that the subject was personally involved in the action of the verb:

寧信度，無自信也。	It is better to trust measurements and not to trust oneself. (55b.4)
貧乏不能自存。	He was impoverished and unable to support himself. (81.1)
先自度其足…	He first measured his feet himself... (55b.1)
人主自用其刑德。	The ruler himself employs his punishments and rewards. (61.3)

Verbs

Verbs may be transitive or intransitive.

I   Causative Verbs:

Verbs may have a causative meaning. This is generally the case when an intransitive verb has an object, e.g., 活, to live, becomes to cause or allow to live, i.e., to save his life, in 活之. Transitive verbs may also have such a meaning, e.g., 飲水, to drink water, but 飲馬, to cause or allow a horse to drink, i.e., to water a horse. In the last example there is a difference in pronunciation: in the first case 飲 is pronounced in the third tone, in the second case in the fourth tone.

II   The Passive Voice:

(a)   The agent of a passive verb may be introduced by 於, e.g., 東敗於齊, in the east I was defeated by Ch'i (22.2), (cf. 東敗齊, in the east I defeated Ch'i); 制於臣, to be ruled by ministers (61.12), (cf. 制臣, to rule ministers).

(b)   見 may be placed before the verb:

百姓之不見保…	That the people were not protected... (28.3)

When the agent is expressed, it is generally introduced by 於, "that the people were not protected by the king" would be 百姓之不見保於王.

(c) The relative pronoun 所 + V may be translated into the passive, e.g., 所見, what is seen. 為 is used to introduce the agent:

先即制人，後則為人所制。	Those who are first will rule others, those who are last will be ruled by others.

Sometimes only 為 is used, e.g., 身為宋國笑, he became a laughing stock in the state of Sung (lit., he was laughed at by the state of Sung), (57.14). Finally the agent is not always expressed, e.g., 為所笑 implies 為之所笑.

(d) When a transitive verb is used intransitively, i.e., without an object, it becomes passive, e.g., 廟成, the ancestral temple was completed (83.22). The verb may be preceded by 可 or 足 (in an active construction 可以 and 足以 are used):

左右皆曰可殺…	If your attendants say he can be killed… (39.10)
仁人也，不可失也。	He is a good man; he cannot be lost. (41.9)
不可再見者，親也。	Those who cannot be seen again are parents. (64.14)
四十，五十而無聞焉，斯亦不足畏也已。	If at forty or fifty nothing [of note] has been heard of him, then surely he is not worth fearing (being taken seriously). (127.10)

III Changes in Word Class:

(a) A verb may be used as an adverb to qualify another verb:

無與立談者。	No one stood (stopped) to talk with him. (3.1)

(b) After a 其 or a 之 verbs become nouns:

見其生，不忍見其死。	If one sees them alive (their life) one cannot bear to see them dead (their death). (27.12)
其曲中規。	Its curve will conform to the compass. (92.3)
善哉！善哉！子之聽夫！	Excellent indeed is your listening! (How well you listen!) (74.7)

Adjectives

Adjectives, both in Classical and Modern Chinese, are classed with verbs.

I Causative and Putative Meaning:

When an adjective is used as a verb it is generally intransitive, e.g., 不遠 means "not to be far". In the phrase 不遠千里, 千里 is the object of 遠; in such cases the adjective becomes a transitive verb with a putative or causative meaning

GRAMMATICAL NOTES

indicating that the object is considered to have the quality expressed by the verb or that the object is caused to have the quality of the verb; the phrase therefore means "not to consider a thousand *li* far" (10.1). A causative usage of 遠 is 是以君子遠庖廚, therefore a gentleman keeps far from (causes to be far) the kitchen (27.13). Another example would be X 小之: X considered it to be small, or X made it small, depending on the context. Some other examples:

老吾老，以及人之老。	Treat the old people of your own family as they ought to be treated and with it reach to the old people of others. (28.10)
大學之道在明明德。	The way of great learning lies in making bright bright virtue. (68.1)

II Changes in Word Class:

An adjective becomes a noun when it is made nominal by 之 or 其, e.g., 明月 means "bright moon", whereas 月之明 means "the brightness of the moon", 白馬 means "white horse", whereas 白馬之白 means "the whiteness of a white horse".

When an adjective is in the position of a subject or an object it indicates a specific person or a group of persons or things, e.g., 老吾老, where the first 老 is a verb and the second a noun: treat as old your own old [people]; another example is:

民扶老攜幼，迎君道中。	The people, supporting the old and leading the young, welcomed the lord on the road. (83.5)

Adjectives become nouns when they follow numerals: 三仁, three benevolent ones; 二老, two old people.

GRAMMATICAL NOTES

Function Words

I 者 *chě*

(a) 者 is a pronominal suffix the function of which is to make the preceding word or phrase nominal. It is qualified by the preceding adjective, verb or predicate and forms a nominal clause: one who (is or does), those who (are or do), thing which (is or does), that which (is or does). Most commonly it will indicate a person but may also indicate a thing or an event. The modern equivalent is 的人(事，東西).

弒其君者…	The one who kills his prince… (10.6)
若寡人者，可以保民乎哉？	Can one who is like me really protect the people? (26.6)
知者不言，言者不知。	Those who know do not speak, those who speak do not know.

(b) 者 may be used in equational sentences: A 者 B 也 = A is B.

南冥者，天池也。	The southern sea is the heavenly pool. (109.4)
謂其君不能者，賊其君也。	The one who says his ruler is not capable, injures his ruler. (49.12)

(c) The pattern 有 + OBJ + 者 means "there are those who"; 未有 + OBJ + 者 "there have never been those who", and 無 + OBJ + 者 "there are not those who".

未有仁而遺其親者。	There has never been one who was good yet neglected his parents. (10.9)
王坐於堂上，有牽牛而過堂下者。	[When] Your Majesty was sitting at the top of the hall, there was one who (someone) led an ox past the bottom of the hall. (26.9)

This pattern is often used to classify the person, thing or event described in the 者 clause, as belonging to a certain group:

宋人有耕田者。	Among the men of Sung there was a farmer. (57.12)
王之臣有託其妻子於其友而之楚遊者。	Among Your Majesty's subjects there was one who entrusted his wife and children to a friend and went on an excursion to Ch'u. (37.1)

GRAMMATICAL NOTES

or as a marker of a subject:

二柄者，刑德也。	The two handles are punishment and favour. (61.1)

(d) When 者 is used after numerals it refers to nouns that have been mentioned previously: 二者, the two, 三者, the three. It may also indicate people's age: 五十者, one who is fifty years old. When it is joined to time words it refers to "time when", e.g., 今者，昔者，古者.

(e) A noun joined to a 者 clause by 之 identifies the group of persons or objects, the place or the time to which the subject of the 者 clause belongs:

天下之刖者多矣。	In the empire those who have had their feet cut off are many. (52.8)
古之欲明明德於天下者。	In ancient times those who wished to make clear bright virtue. (68.4)

This pattern may also indicate the superlative:

齊國之美麗者。	The most handsome one in the state of Ch'i (lit., The one who is handsome in the state of Ch'i). (78.3)
晏嬰，齊之習辭者也。	Yen Ying is the most eloquent person in Ch'i. (71.1)

The correct interpretation depends on the context of the passage.

II   之 *chīh*

(a)   As a verb it means "to go"

牛何之？	Where is the ox going? (26.10)
從良人之所之。	She followed wherever her husband went. (3.1)
之祭者，乞其餘。	He went up to those offering sacrifices and begged for leftovers. (3.2)

(b) A demonstrative adjective equivalent to the modern 這: 之子 "this man".

之二蟲，又何知？	These two creatures, what do they know? (109.17)

(c) Pronoun object: him, her, it, them, equivalent to the modern 他, 他們, 她, 她們, 它 used as objects. In this usage it stands after the verb or preposition, except in sentences containing a negative adverb:

寡人恥之。	I am ashamed of it. (22.3)
王見之。	The king saw him. (26.10)
乃屬其耆老而告之…	He then assembled the elders and told them… (41.5)

臣未之聞也。	I have never heard it. (26.3)
王往而征之。	Your Majesty, go and subjugate them. (22.10)

When the topical subject is the grammatical object of the verb it is often resumed by 之:

恭敬之心，人皆有之。	A respectful heart, all men have it.
青，取之於藍。	Blue comes from indigo. (Blue, take it from indigo), (92.1)
殺戮之謂刑。	Public execution, it is called punishment. (61.2)

(d) Subordinating conjunction joining an attribute to the noun used to indicate possession or to form a relative clause, equivalent to the modern 的:

鄰國之政。	The government of neighbouring states. (13.3)
王道之始。	The beginning of the royal way. (14.5)
饜足之道也。	The way in which he was satisfied (ate well). (3.3)
謹庠序之教。	Be careful about the teaching in schools. (14.9)

(e) Used to transform S + P into a nominal clause:

人性善→人性之善也，猶水之就下也。	Human nature is good. → Human nature is good like water flowing downwards. (44.5)
無望民之多於鄰國。	Do not expect that your people will be more numerous than those in neighbouring states. (14.1)
人性之無分於善不善，猶水之無分於東西也。	Man's nature does not distinguish between good and bad, just as water does not distinguish between east and west. (44.2)
察鄰國之政，無如寡人之用心者。	When I examine the governments of neighbouring states, there is no-one equal to me in using the heart. (13.3)

III 諸 *chū* is a fusion of PRON OBJ 之 + PREP 於, or PRON 之 + INT PART 乎.

(a) In the first case 諸 occurs in a post-verbal position and the following word is the object of the preposition:

舉斯心加諸彼。	He raised these feelings and applied them to others. (28.12)
吾聞諸夫子。	I heard it from the master.

GRAMMATICAL NOTES

性猶湍水也，決諸東方則東流，決諸西方則西流。	Human nature is like rushing water: if an opening is made to the east it will flow east, and if an opening is made to the west it will flow west. (44.1)

(b)   In the second case it occurs at the end of a sentence:

不識有諸？	I do not know whether this was so? (26.13)
文王之囿方七十里，有諸？	King Wen's park was 70 *li* square—was it so? (35.1)

(c)   諸 is also an adjective, "all, various" and is often used to indicate the plural:

諸大夫皆曰…	The great officers all say… (39.6)
問門下諸客…	He asked the retainers… (81.16)

IV   而 *érh* is a conjunction.

(a)   Coordinating (i.e., and) or adversative (i.e., but, yet) conjunction. It does not join nouns or nominal clauses. It often has a subordinating function indicating that the main verb occurs under the circumstances presented in the subordinate clause. Thus the clause preceding 而 has the function of an adverbial modifier of the main verb indicating the way in which something is done or the sequence in which it is done.

Coordinating:

人民少而禽獸眾。	People were few and birds and beasts were many. (57.1)
後義而先利。	To put righteousness last and put profit first. (10.8)

Adversative:

未有仁而遺其親者也。	There has never yet been one who was good yet neglected his parents. (10.9)
吾力足以舉百鈞，而不足以舉一羽。	My strength is sufficient to lift one hundred catties, but not sufficient to lift a single feather. (27.18)

Subordinating:

棄甲曳兵而走。	Abandoning their armour and trailing their weapons, they fled. (13.6)
保民而王。	Rule by protecting the people. (26.5)
生而同聲	They are born making the same sounds. (92.8)

吾五十而知天命。	When I was 50 I knew Heaven's mandate. (126.4)

(b) 而 joins adverbs of time to the verb:

晨而求見。	In the morning, he sought an audience. (82.14)
今一朝而鬻技百金。	Now in one morning, we can sell the recipe for 100 pieces of gold. (114.8)

(c) 而 may also be used to join two independent clauses, with the force of "and also", "moreover", "and then":

王以和為誑，而刖其左足。	The king thought Ho was deceiving him, so he had his left foot cut off. (52.2)
先自度其足而置之其坐。	First he himself measured his feet and then placed it (i.e., the measurement) on the seat. (55b.1)

V 以 *i* is a verb meaning "to use", "to take", etc. As a function word it may be used as follows:

(a) Instrumental preposition, i.e., the means by which something is done: with, by, through, on account of, because of, according to. The pattern is 以 + OBJ + V + OBJ or V + OBJ + 以 + OBJ. When the object of the preposition is the pronoun object 之 it is generally omitted.

請以戰喻。	Allow me to illustrate by means of war. (13.5)
樹之以桑。	Plant it with mulberry. (14.7)
斧斤以時入山林。	Take axes into the mountain forests at the right time. (14.3)
左右以君賤之，食以草具。	The attendants, because the ruler looked down upon him, fed him with coarse food. (81.5)

(b) 以 may be translated "to regard as", "to consider". In this meaning it is often used in conjunction with 為. The common patterns are: 以 A 為 B, to take A and make it B, i.e., to regard A as B; 以(之)為 B, to regard (it) as B; and 以為 B, to consider B:

民猶以為小。	The people still consider [it] to be small. (35.4)
孔子以魯小 。	Confucius considered Lu to be small.
王以和為誑。	The king thought Ho was deceiving [him]. (52.2)
百姓皆以王為愛也。	The people thought Your Majesty was grudging. (27.1)

GRAMMATICAL NOTES

The pattern 以 A 為 B may also be used to mean "use A to make B", e.g., 何不慮以為大樽, Why did you not think of making [it] into a large goblet? (114.12)

(c)　Conjunction: in order to. 以 is used between two verbal clauses to show that what is expressed by the second action is the outcome of the first action, i.e., it indicates the method, means or reason for the action of the second verb:

竭力以事大國。	I exert my strength in order to serve large states. (41.1)
構木為巢以避群害。	He put up frames of wood to make nests in order to escape all harm. (57.2)

(d)　It links time and position words with nouns:

三代以前	Before the Three Dynasties.
由山以上五六里	Five or six *li* up the mountain.

VI　然 *ján* means "to be so, thus" and may be used as follows:

(a)　To express agreement: yes, it is so:

然；誠有百姓者。	Yes; truly there are such people. (27.3)

(b)　As a clause connecting what has been said in the previous sentence to the clause that follows it. Thus 然則 means "if it is so, then,"; 雖然 means "even though it is so, nevertheless, however":

然則廢釁鐘與？	If it is so, are we to give up consecrating the bell? (26.12)
然則一羽之不舉，為不用力焉。	If so, then a feather not being lifted is [a case of] not using strength at it. (28.2)
雖然，臣之質死久矣。	However, my subject has been dead for a long time. (102a.5)
然非喪者之哀也。	However, it is not the grief of a mourner. (64.2)

(c)　Used in combination with 後, it is used to indicate time sequence between two clauses, showing that the action of the final clause can happen only after the action of the first clause has been completed:

臣始至於境，問國之大禁，然後敢入。	When I arrived at the border, I asked about the important prohibitions of the state before I dared enter. (35.8)
權，然後知輕重。	Weigh them, and afterwards you will know which is light and which is heavy. (28.16)

(d) Placed after an adjective it is an adverbial suffix, like the English "-ly":

填然鼓之。	With a boom (lit., boomingly), roused them to action. (13.5)
非不喝然大也。	It is not that they were not enormously big. (114.3)

VII 所 *sŏ* is a relative pronoun indicating a person, event or thing: what, that which, which. It serves as the object of the verb or preposition, which it precedes; because a 所 + V phrase is in Classical Chinese nominal, there will generally be a 之 after the noun in a 所 clause and often a 者 at the end of the clause. 所 + VT may be translated into the English passive.

Some examples of the use of 所:

叟之所知也。	It is what you, Sir, know. (22.1)
伯牙所念…	Whatever Po-ya thought of… (74.4)
見吾家所寡有者。	See what my house lacks. (82.11)
所謂故國者。	What is called an ancient state. (39.1)
臣之所好者，道也。	What I care about is the Way. (106.5)
魚，我所欲也，熊掌，亦我所欲也。	A fish is what I desire, and a bear's paw is also what I desire. (46.1)

所 is indefinite, unspecific, but it can be made specific by a noun placed after the 所 phrase, which may be linked to it by 之. In this case the 所 phrase qualifies the noun:

籍所殺之漢軍。	The Han army that was slaughtered by Chi.

者 may be placed after 所 + V to replace a specific noun and thus form a nominal clause:

狄人之所欲者。	What the barbarians desire. (41.6)
其妻問所與飲食者。	His wife asked with whom he ate and drank. (2.2)
所惡有甚於死者。	Among the things I hate, there are some things [I hate] more than death. (46.5)

VIII 所以 *sŏ-ĭ*, that with which, the reason why, the means by which.

The difference between 所 and 所以 may be illustrated by the following examples:

其所知	what he knows
其所以知	the means by which he knows

GRAMMATICAL NOTES

Some examples:

其所以聖。	The reason why he is a sage.
乃臣所以為君市義。	This was the means by which I bought righteousness for you. (83.2)
此吾所以悲也。	This is the reason I am sad. (52.10)
君子不以其所以養人者害人。	The gentleman does not, by means of what he uses to nourish others, harm others. (41.6)
古之人所以大過人者。	The reason why men of ancient times greatly surpassed others. (28.13)
人之所以求富貴利達者。	The means by which men seek riches and honour, profit and success. (3.7)
此心之所以合於王者，何也？	How is this heart (lit., the means by which this heart) compatible with being a king? (27.16)

IX 則 *tsé* then, indicates that the action in the main clause can only happen as a result of the action or condition presented in the subordinate clause.

(a) 則 often gives a conditional or temporal force, i.e., "if" or "when" to the sentence, i.e., the first clause produces the condition or reason under which the second clause may occur.

河內凶則移其民於河東。	When/if there is a disaster in Ho-nei, I move the people to Ho-tung. (13.2)
決諸東方則東流。	If one makes an opening to the east, it will flow east. (44.1)

(b) It may also refer to a recurrent event or a habitual action:

其良人出，則必饜酒肉而後反。	Whenever the husband went out, he always returned home having eaten and drunk well. (2.1)

(c) 則 may sometimes be used to mark off a subject, giving it slight emphasis:

臣則嘗能斵之。	I used to be able to slice it off. (102a.5)

X 為 *wéi*

(a) 為 is used as the copula verb "to be", and has the additional meanings: act as, constitute, effect, make, do, consider, etc. For example:

冰，水為之。	Ice is made of water. (92.2)
北冥有魚，其名為鯤。	In the north sea there is a fish; its name is K'un. (109.1)

寡人不敢以先王之臣為臣。	I do not dare use a minister of the former king as a minister. (83.4)
以故相為上將軍。	He made the former prime minister (to be) the commander-in-chief. (83.12)
不為不多。	Cannot be considered as little. (10.8)
王之不王，不為也。	A king's not being a king is [a case of] not acting. (28.4)
是方四十里為阱於國中。	This forty *li* square is a trap in the middle of the kingdom. (35.10)

(b) One pattern to express the passive is: 為 + N + (所) + V in which 為 introduces the agent for the verb, and 所 is the object of the passive verb:

宋為楚所敗於吳。	Sung was defeated by Ch'u in Wu.
為其友所知。	Came to be known by his friend.

XI 為 *wèi* for, on behalf of, for the sake of, because of. 為 takes the normal position of a preposition: 為 + OBJ + V + OBJ:

為長者折枝。	To break a branch for an elder. (28.7)
庖丁為文惠君解牛。	Cook Ting carved an ox for Lord Wen-hui. (106.1)

XII 也 *yěh* affirms the construction that precedes it.

(a) The commonest use of 也 is as a marker of a nominal predicate: A B 也 = A is B. Some examples:

此其為饜足之道也。	This was the way he satisfied himself. (3.3)
此人主失刑德之患也。	This is the calamity of a ruler losing (control over) punishment and reward. (61.8)
是乃仁術也。	This is in fact an artifice of goodness. (27.11)
南冥者，天池也。	The southern sea is the heavenly pool. (109.4)

(b) 也 may be used to indicate a pause after a subject, thus stressing it:

斯道也，何道也？	What kind of way is this? (lit., This way is what kind of way?)

(c) Equational sentences using 也 are often used to express a cause or reason for something:

妾之美我者畏我也。	My concubine considers me handsome because she stands in awe of me. (78.10)

GRAMMATICAL NOTES

孟嘗君為相數十年⋯者，馮諼之計也。	That Lord Meng-ch'ang was minister for several tens of years... was because of Feng Hsüan's plan. (83.24)

(d) It may also be used in questions:

寡人之民不加多，何也？	My people do not increase—why? (13.4)

(e) When 也 is used as a final particle in a narrative sentence it affirms or emphasizes the statement that precedes it:

仁人也，不可失也。	He is a benevolent man; he cannot be lost. (41.9)
君曰：客何好。曰：客無好也。	The lord said: "What does the guest like?" He said: "The guest has no likes." (81.2)

XIII 焉 yēn

(a) 焉 is a fusion of 於 + 之, i.e., PREP + PRON OBJ: at it, on it, from it, than it, etc. It is used after a verb or adjective and its position is at the end of the clause.

晉國，天下莫強焉。	The state of Chin—none in the world is stronger than it. (22.1)
寡人之於國也，盡心焉耳矣。	My attitude towards my country is that I exert my whole mind for it and that is all. (13.1)
牛羊何擇焉？	An ox and a sheep—how can you choose between them? (27.7)
置杯焉則膠，水淺而舟大也。	If you place a cup in it, it will stick, for the water is shallow and the boat is large. (109.10)

(b) 焉 is also an interrogative adverb: how, why, where. In this usage its position is at the head of the clause before the verb:

後生可畏，焉知來者之不如今也？	Respect the young, how do you know that in the future they will not equal those of the present? (127.9)
焉用亡秦以陪鄰？	What use is it to destroy Ch'in to add to your neighbour? (134.10)

XIV 於 yú

於 indicates a relationship between two words without specifying the exact relationship.

(a)   It may introduce a complement indicating location, direction, time, etc., and be translated by a preposition: in, on, from, at, to, etc. The pattern is S + V + (OBJ) + 於 + OBJ:

移其民於河東。	I move the people to Ho-tung. (13.2)
王如施仁政於民…	If Your Majesty extends benevolent government to the people… (22.5)
王請擇於斯二者。	Your Majesty, please choose between these two things. (41.12)
而相泣於中庭。	And they wept together in the courtyard. (3.5)
夫子固拙於用大矣。	You are truly clumsy at using large things. (114.5)

Occasionally, 於 and its object are placed at the beginning of the sentence:

於我心有戚戚焉。	In my heart there was a feeling of sympathy for it. (27.16)
於傳有之。	In the records it is so. (35.2)

(b)   After an adjective 於 introduces the object of comparison:

無望民之多於鄰國也。	Do not expect that your people will be more numerous than those in neighbouring states. (14.1)
青,取之於藍,而青於藍。	Blue comes from indigo, but it is bluer than indigo. (92.1)
皆以美於徐公。	All considered me more handsome than Mr Hsü. (78.14)
天下莫強焉。(焉 = 於之)	In the world, none is stronger than it. (22.1)

(c)   於 introduces the agent of a passive verb:

東敗於齊… 南辱於楚。	In the east I was defeated by Ch'i… in the south I was disgraced by Ch'u. (22.2)
愛於人。	To be loved by others.

(d)   Used between two nouns 於 indicates attitude towards or relationship to:

寡人之於國也。	My attitude towards my country. (13.1)
君子之於禽獸也。	A gentleman's attitude to animals. (27.12)

Index

This index is arranged according to the number of strokes in a character, and each group of numbers is further sub-divided into five sections: 一, 丨, 丿, 丶, and 乛, i.e., the first stroke of each character. The examples below will make the arrangement clear. The numbers refer to the page on which the character may be found.

一	丁	未	墦	樹	薄	聽
丨	上	日	數	對	馳	黨
丿	人	乞	川	凡	手	顧
丶	之	心	火	忖	彰	鄰
乛	又	已	母	能	崇	經
	水	習	陰	婦	孟	門

2-4 Strokes

2 Strokes

一	丁	107				
丿	人	4	入	18	乃	31
乛	又	7	力	32	刀	107

3 Strokes

一	大	11	士	11	下	12
	于	33	才	40	土	42
	干	94	寸	96	工	120
	丈	128				
丨	上	12	山	18	口	19
	小	31	巾	103		
丿	乞	7	千	11		
	凡	47	久	103	川	118
	夕	128	勺	139		
丶	之	6	亡	40		
乛	子	4	也	5	已	11
	刃	17	己	62		

4 Strokes

一	不	7	王	11	夫	11
	木	18	天	21	比	23
	云	32	太	33	友	38
	犬	42	井	50	牙	62
	元	103	匹	113		

168

4-5 Strokes

丨	日	5	中	6	內	16
	少	16	止	17	日	24
ノ	反	5	今	8	仁	11
	凶	16	斤	18	勿	19
	及	23	父	24	牛	30
	公	42	分	45	乏	48
	氏	53	化	59	爪	62
	兮	75	月	80	介	88
	手	107	夭	112	什	132
丶	心	16	方	23	文	29
	火	50	斗	118		
ㄱ	以	9	予	32	水	45
	孔	65	尺	79		

5 Strokes

一	未	5	可	17	世	29
	末	33	功	33	古	34
	左	38	右	38	去	40
	玉	42	本	48	石	53
	平	66	正	69	示	118
	巧	120	甘	132		
丨	出	4	由	9	甲	17
	田	19	申	20	兄	24
	北	33	且	56	旦	79
	目	108	史	120		
ノ	他	7	外	8	乎	11
	用	16	生	18	失	19
	白	20	乍	50	令	80
	仞	96	代	105	斥	113
	冬	115	丘	118	仕	129
	犯	137				
丶	必	4	立	6	市	43
	主	62	玄	120	氾	136
ㄱ	民	16	加	16	母	25
	尼	29	幼	33	皮	42
	弗	47	矛	56	召	86

6 Strokes

一	有	4	而	4	百	12

INDEX

6-7 Strokes

一	耳	16	死	18	至	21
	西	23	地	23	刑	24
	臣	29	老	33	在	45
	再	66	吏	72	列	75
	存	84	成	88	夷	95
	共	95	匠	103	朴	119
	戎	137				
丨	肉	4	此	7	曳	17
	同	36	因	60	曲	76
	早	136				
丿	仰	7	危	12	多	12
	先	12	仲	29	行	32
	合	32	自	50	刖	53
	血	53	名	54	伐	59
	后	59	耒	60	年	66
	似	72	廷	80	休	87
	舟	95	全	105	色	111
	朱	119	伏	139		
丶	亦	11	交	12	池	18
	宅	19	衣	19	羊	30
	忖	32	守	43	充	50
	安	69	江	75	冰	94
	汝	105	次	128		
𠃌	如	16	好	16	羽	32
	收	85				

7 Strokes

一	吾	6	求	9	走	17
	材	18	孝	20	否	33
	形	33	折	33	豆	47
	車	65	投	66	戒	66
	志	75	更	76	扶	87
	芷	97	邪	97	技	107
	批	108	芥	112	杖	128
	芸	129	李	136	杞	137
	克	139				
丨	足	7	見	11	里	11
	步	17	邑	42	岐	42

INDEX

7-8 Strokes

丨	肖	101	吹	111	吳	115
	困	137				
ノ	告	5	身	8	利	9
	希	9	何	11	兵	17
	我	20	坐	29	邦	34
	免	42	邪	42	狄	42
	位	53	作	58	伯	75
	每	76	私	80	卵	96
	角	113	谷	118	含	119
	佚	136	孚	139		
丶	良	4	序	19	弟	25
	言	32	決	45	忘	56
	宋	60	初	75	沉	85
	完	96				
乛	君	9	矣	9	壯	24
	忍	30	即	31	阱	36
	忌	79	防	97	尾	103
	改	128				

8 Strokes

一	妻	4	者	4	其	4
	來	6	東	6	若	8
	取	12	苟	12	或	17
	直	17	林	18	刺	21
	事	24	枝	33	昔	40
	奉	48	武	53	抱	53
	雨	75	到	86	奈	86
	拊	86	枕	87	臥	87
	青	94	招	95	苕	96
	茂	100	杯	112	坳	112
	枋	112	拙	115	松	128
	函	136				
丨	長	23	易	24	忠	24
	固	30	明	32	呼	47
	果	58	虎	62	味	72
	具	84	肯	100	唱	115
ノ	所	5	知	8	征	12
	斧	18	使	18	帛	19

171

INDEX

8-9 Strokes

ノ	狗	19	非	20	制	25
	彼	25	往	25	舍	30
	物	34	兔	36	卑	40
	受	47	朋	50	和	53
	命	54	近	59	周	59
	服	62	邱	65	念	75
	迎	87	金	87	狐	90
	肩	107	依	108	委	108
	垂	111	爭	119	采	119
	季	128	版	137		
丶	妾	4	卒	6	泣	8
	於	8	河	16	宜	31
	庖	31	治	38	性	45
	怳	50	夜	53	法	60
	定	69	怪	85	券	86
	放	87	宗	88	官	108
	況	108	並	118	沛	128
	沽	128				
ㄱ	孟	4	始	19	姓	30
	居	42	門	80	姑	88

9 Strokes

一	相	8	政	16	南	23
	故	25	哉	29	胡	29
	皆	30	甚	34	要	50
	持	56	柄	62	威	62
	厚	66	春	72	枳	72
	耶	72	奏	76	城	79
	面	80	草	84	柱	84
	契	86	珍	86	封	88
	荊	90	荀	94	指	120
	柏	128	拱	129		
丨	則	4	是	17	省	24
	囿	36	貞	54	胃	59
	畏	62	思	65	曷	72
	映	79	昭	90	昨	100
	背	111	削	120		
ノ	後	5	食	5	負	20

9-10 Strokes

ノ							
	信	24	保	29	秋	32
	重	34	侵	42	泉	50
	禹	59	風	66	待	66
	狡	87	侯	87	俗	95
	竿	103	眷	107	胠	118
	律	119	竽	119	矩	119
	急	136	牲	139		
、	室	4	施	6, 8	為	7
	洿	18	庠	19	洒	23
	宣	29	度	32	郊	36
	美	48	音	65	哀	65
	前	65	洋	75	冠	79
	客	79	計	85	軍	87
	恤	90	帝	90	恆	95
	神	95	祖	101	首	107
	恢	108	洴	115	恃	132
ㄱ	既	17	紂	59	姦	62
	約	85	飛	105	怒	111
	陋	128	勇	139	盈	139

10 Strokes

一							
	起	6	荸	20	晉	23
	莫	23	秦	23	辱	23
	恥	23	桓	29	挾	33
	珠	42	耆	42	夏	59
	株	60	致	65	索	65
	格	69	泰	75	恐	87
	破	96	莖	96	根	97
	莊	100	挫	101	埃	111
	莽	112	軒	118	貢	128
	荷	128				
丨	時	17	罟	18	財	31
	恩	33	馬	42	豈	45
	哭	53	蚌	58	晏	72
	峨	75	畢	86	鄡	103
	骨	103				
ノ	叟	11	乘	12	笑	17
	飢	19	殺	21	耕	24

INDEX

10-11 Strokes

ノ	修	24	徒	29	芻	36
	師	38	奚	53	臭	58
	桀	59	殷	59	追	65
	逃	76	徐	79	倚	84
	倦	85	息	95	射	96
	俱	100	倫	101	鬼	103
	留	103	邠	108	特	113
	氣	113	倕	120		
丶	酒	4	訕	8	庭	8
	家	11	歔	19	畜	19
	悌	20	凍	25	海	33
	託	38	害	42	效	43
	流	45	兼	47	宮	47
	悦	58	疾	59	病	59
	悔	65	記	69	席	72
	高	75	祥	88	被	88
	逆	90	旁	100	浮	100
	送	103	容	103	冥	111
	朔	113	剖	115	悖	124
	益	136	衰	139		
ㄱ	蚤	6	桑	19	能	29
	屑	47	書	80	崇	88
	孫	124				
11 Strokes						
一	焉	12	接	17	教	19
	梃	25	堅	25	戚	32
	推	34	理	54	帶	65
	奢	66	責	85	區	86
	專	90	規	94	挺	94
	盛	100	堊	103	梧桐	105
	硎	108	培	112	控	112
	春	112	菌	112	瓠	115
	掊	115	逐	118	逝	128
	執	136	曹	139		
丨	處	4	國	6	異	20
	敗	23	堂	29	患	42
	眾	58	蛇	58	常	60

11-12 Strokes

丨	晚	65	崩	76	晨	86
	趺	95	累	100	唯	101
	逍	111	野	111	晦	113
	冕	118				
ノ	從	6	祭	7	移	16
	魚	18	豚	19	得	25
	術	31	欲	42	停	66
	逢	75	造	76	策	79
	貧	84	貪	84	悉	86
	假	95	鳥	96	釣	103
	笥	103	動	108	徙	111
	斛	118	符	118	脫	118
	彫	128				
丶	郭	7	望	8	羞	9
	梁	11	庶	12	深	24
	牽	30	毫	32	許	33
	鹿	36	惕	50	視	72
	淮	72	孰	79	寄	84
	麻	97	烹	100	情	101
	族	108	淺	112	宿	112
	章	119	康	128	設	137
ㄱ	問	5	將	6	終	8
	強	23	陷	25	巢	58
	習	72	陰	75	婦	80
	項	84	陳	86	參	94
	晝	128	陵	136	陪	136

12 Strokes

一	惠	11	萬	12	粟	16
	喪	18	斯	21	壹	23
	散	25	惡	31	超	33
	敢	36	堯	59	期	60
	酣	72	葉	72	琴	75
	援	75	朝	79	揭	84
	黃	87	報	88	博	94
	越	94	葦	96	喜	100
	雁	100	欺	101	葬	103
	搜	105	軱	108	提	108

INDEX

12-13 Strokes

一	雲	111	極	111	彭	113
	棘	113	落	115	裂	115
	焚	119	殘	119	惑	120
	棺	124	敬	128	植	129
	貳	136				
丨	貴	5	喻	17	掌	33
	蛤	58	虛	87	景	95
	量	100	貽	115	買	115
	跖	118	黑	124	圍	136
	敝	137				
丿	飲	5	無	6	弒	12
	然	16	勝	17	稅	24
	禽	31	復	32	鈞	32
	御	34	短	34	猶	36
	喬	40	進	40	智	50
	悲	53	舜	59	備	60
	象	76	傅	87	須	95
	順	95	循	105	黍	129
	焦	137				
丶	富	5	棄	17	寒	20
	就	30	善	34	尊	40
	湍	45	惻	50	湯	59
	盜	72	游	75	馮	84
	廄	86	淵	96	割	108
	翔	113	湖	115	曾	120
	測	139				
乛	閑	7	幾	9	發	20
	疏	40	鄉	48	絕	66
	登	75	給	85	開	85
	統	88	間	100	絨	115
	結	132				

13 Strokes

一	達	9	填	17	鼓	17
	楚	23	禁	36	搏	45
	勢	45	楯	56	聖	58
	構	58	蒜	58	想	76
	載	85	賈	86	聘	87

13-14 Strokes

一	楫	96	蒙	96	蓬	96
	墓	103	蓋	107	搖	111
	蒼	111	榆	112	椿	113
	蒿	113	瑟	119	楊	120
	葆	129	勤	129	瑕	137
	肆	137	軾	139		
丨	農	17	路	20	歲	20
	罪	21	暇	24	過	30
	賊	50	置	56	號	58
	當	60	暑	85	愚	85
	嗟	95	嘗	100	遇	107
	盟	137	馳	139		
丿	與	5	遍	6	尟	19
	頒	20	傳	29	愛	30
	傷	31	雉	36	腥	58
	腹	59	亂	59	節	66
	鄒	79	會	85	僅	87
	貉	95	鳩	96	毀	101
	鼠	105	解	107	微	108
	鉤	118	鈸	118	鉗	120
	傾	132				
丶	道	7	義	11	塗	20
	溺	25	誠	30	詩	32
	運	33	遊	38	慎	40
	遂	54	試	56	新	60
	誅	62	意	69	詣	72
	窟	87	禍	88	靖	95
	福	95	廉	101	塞	119
	滅	119	慈	128	煩	136
ㄱ	違	17	辟	47	群	58
	裝	85	經	107		

14 Strokes

一	遠	11	奪	12	輕	34
	境	36	爾	47	厲	53
	熙	72	輒	76	暮	79
	趙	80	歌	84	槁	94
	槐	97	搏	111	槍	112

INDEX

14-15 Strokes

一		聚	112	厭	137		
｜		嘗	5	對	11	罰	24
		嘆	76	遣	87	鳴	100
		圖	112	蜩	112	鄙	119
ノ		疑	25	僕	65	貌	79
		稱	86	鼻	103	舞	107
		緊	108	遙	111	種	115
		僖	136	獄	139		
、		齊	4	寡	16	察	16
		福	31	說	31	語	33
		竭	42	端	50	誕	53
		寧	56	實	72	寢	79
		誠	87	彰	95	漸	97
		滸	97	慢	103	腐	105
		滿	108	塵	111	旗	139
乛		盡	5	聞	29	熊	47

15 Strokes

一		墦	7	穀	17	堯	36
		賢	40	趣	76	蔽	80
		憂	85	輪	94	豎	100
		槨	124				
｜		數	18	幣	42	罷	56
		暴	59	賞	62	慮	69
		賜	72	賤	84	駟	88
		髮	96	踦	107	墨	120
		劌	139				
ノ		餘	7	黎	20	餓	20
		德	29	餒	38	滕	42
		劍	84	鋏	84	質	97
		僻	97	斷	103	膝	107
		膠	112	箴	118		
、		談	6	鄰	16	請	16
		養	18	誰	25	敵	25
		廢	30	諸	30	廚	31
		窮	48	鄭	56	論	60
		慶	62	適	65	諾	84
		憤	85	廟	88	諂	88

15-17 Strokes

、	諛	88	廣	113	審	124
	潔	129				
ㄱ	履	56	毅	62	彈	84
	駕	84	樂	88	編	96
	練	105	槳	115	縋	136

16 Strokes

一	樹	19	薄	24	撻	25
	擇	31	薪	33	璞	53
	蕘	53	操	56	頸	60
	擁	65	靜	66	橘	72
	霖	75	燕	80	薛	85
	輮	94	瓢	115	樽	115
	殫	119	整	137		
丨	遺	12	戰	16	踰	40
	冀	60	器	88	餐	112
ノ	耨	24	舉	32	獨	33
	學	66	積	86	鴟	105
	龜	103, 115	翱	113	衡	118
、	親	12	憾	18	謂	31
	激	45	導	62	窺	79
	諫	80	護	84	燒	86
	隨	90	謀	101	遲	108
	諧	111	澼	115		
ㄱ	縛	72	關	112		

17 Strokes

一	戴	20	檢	20	觳	30
	聲	31	輿	33	韓	53
	藍	94	臨	94	藏	103
	擊	111	擢	119	聰	119
丨	瞷	6	雖	31	還	66
	嬰	72	虧	101	嚇	105
ノ	斂	24	禦	29	鍾	47
	儲	56	臊	58	償	86
	矯	86	谿	94		
、	麋	36	禮	47	應	56
	燧	59	謗	80	謝	85
	懧	85	龍	100	濮	103

179

INDEX

17-20 Strokes

、	濠	105	歜	108	謙	108
	燭	136	濟	137		
ㄱ	隱	31	孺	50	避	58
	臂	95	翼	103	績	139

18 Strokes

一	擴	50	覆	111	藥	115
	擷	118	瞽	119		
丨	鼕	29	題	54	蟲	58
	蟪蛄	113				
ノ	歸	7	雞	19	簞	47
	鯀	59	魏	80	儵	105
、	謹	19	瀆	59	糧	112
ㄱ	璧	54	嚮	107	闕	137

19 Strokes

一	願	23	離	25	難	56
	麗	79	勸	94	礪	94
	繫	96	璽	118	顛	128
	櫝	128	轍	139		
丨	獸	31	蹴	47	蠅	103
	驁	107	曠	119		
ノ	辭	50	鏡	79	鯤	111
	鵬	111				
、	識	30	類	33	羹	47
	譏	80	鶉鷃	105	禧	107
	靡	139				
ㄱ	關	36	穎	45	繩	94
	韜	128				

20 Strokes

一	蘭	97	醴	105	攘	120
丨	黨	50	獻	53		
ノ	鐘	30	譽	50	觸	60
	釋	60	覺	65	騰	113
	犧	139				
、	寶	53	議	101		
ㄱ	繼	53				

21-28 Strokes

21 Strokes							
一	權	34	攜	87		
丨	躍	45	驅	65	躊躇	108
	鶼	113				
丿	顧	7	鐮	65		
丶	辯	47	懼	87	齎	88
	爛	120				
乛	屬	42				
22 Strokes						
一	鼇	4	聽	40	攞	120
丨	驕	8				
丶	竊	86				
乛	響	56				
23 Strokes						
丨	顯	5	體	50	巖	75
丿	鑠	119				
丶	鷩	18				
乛	纖	88				
24 Strokes						
一	觀	9	蠹	58	靈	113
丶	讓	50				
26 Strokes						
丿	釁	30				
27 Strokes						
丿	鑽	59				
28 Strokes						
丨	鑿	87				

WILD PEONY PTY LTD BOOK PUBLISHERS A.C.N. 002 714 276
PO BOX 636 BROADWAY NSW 2007 AUSTRALIA
Fax: 61 2 9566 1052

International Distribution: University of Hawaii Press, 2840 Kolowalu Street, Honolulu Hawaii 96822. Fax: 1 808 988-6052

• *Shijin: Autobiography of the Poet Kaneko Mitsuharu, 1895-1975*. Introduction and Translations by A. R. Davis; edited by A. D. Syrokomla-Stefanowska. University of Sydney East Asian Series, No. 1; ISBN: 0 9590735 3 1; 1988; 324pp; hardcover: AUS $40.00

• Tanizaki Jun'ichiro, *A Cat, Shozo and Two Women*. Translated by Matsui Sakuko. University of Sydney East Asian Series, No. 2; ISBN: 0 9590735 5 8; 150pp; 1988; hardcover: AUS $27.95; softcover: AUS $12.95. NOT FOR SALE IN THE USA, CANADA AND UK.

• Yang Lian, *Masks and Crocodile: A Contemporary Chinese Poet and His Poetry*. Introduction and Translations by Mabel Lee; 12 coloured illustrations by Li Liang. University of Sydney East Asian Series, No. 3; ISBN: 0 9590735 7 4; 1990; 146pp; softcover: AUS $25.00

• *Gen'ei: Selected Poems of Nishiwaki Junzaburo, 1894-1982*. Translations by Yasuko Claremont. University of Sydney East Asian Series, No. 4; ISBN: 0 9590735 8 2; 1991; 120pp; softcover: AUS $19.95

• *Seven Stories of Modern Japan*. Edited by Leith Morton. Translations by H. Clarke, S. Matsui and L. Morton. University of Sydney East Asian Series, No. 5; ISBN: 0 9590735 9 0; 1991; 88pp; softcover: AUS $19.95

• *Kyunyŏ-jŏn: The Life, Times and Songs of a Tenth Century Korean Buddhist Monk*. Translated and annotated by Adrian Buzo and Tony Prince. University of Sydney East Asian Series, No. 6; ISBN: 0 646 14772 2; 1993; 142pp; softcover: AUS $25.00

• *Modernity in Asian Art*. Edited by John Clark. University of Sydney East Asian Series, No. 7; ISBN: 0 646 14773 0; 1993; 350pp; softcover: AUS $37.50

• *The Chinese Femme Fatale: Short Stories of the Ming Period*. Translations by Anne McLaren. University of Sydney East Asian Series, No. 8; ISBN: 0 646 14924 5; 1994; 102pp; softcover: AUS $22.95

• *Visiting the Mino Kilns*. Translation and introduction by Janet Barriskill. University of Sydney East Asian Series, No. 9; ISBN: 0-646-20424-6; 1995; 90pp + colour plates 56pp; hardcover: AUS $65.00

Mark Elvin, *Another History: Essays on China from a European Perspective*. University of Sydney East Asian Series No. 10; ISBN: 0 646 20413 0; 1996; 300pp. approx. AUS $40.00

• Mabel Lee and Meng Hua, *Cultural Dialogue and Misreading*. University of Sydney World Literature Series No. 1; ISBN: 0 9586526 1 9; 1996; 500pp; softcover: AUS $45.00

• Mabel Lee and A. D. Syrokomla-Stefanowska (eds), *Modernization of the Chinese Past*; University of Sydney School of Asian Studies Series, No. 1; ISBN: 0 867 58658 3; 1993; 208pp; softcover: AUS $25.00

• Kam Louie, *Between Fact and Fiction: Essays on Post-Mao Literature and Society*; ISBN: 0 9590735 6 6; 1989; 149pp; softcover: AUS $22.75

• Lily Xiao Hong Lee, *The Virtue of Yin: Studies on Chinese Women*; ISBN 0 646 14925 3; 1994; 117pp; softcover: AUS $18.95

• A. D. Syrokomla-Stefanowska, *A Classical Chinese Reader*, ISBN: 0 9586526 0 0; 192 pp; softcover: AUS $40.00

• Mabel Lee and Zhang Wu-ai, *Putonghua: A Practical Course in Spoken Chinese*; ISBN: 0 9590735 0 7; 1984, 1989, 1992; 101pp; softcover: AUS $16.99. [Cassettes available from The Language Centre, University of Sydney NSW 2006, Australia]

• A. D. Syrokomla-Stefanowska and Mabel Lee, *Basic Chinese Grammar and Sentence Patterns*; ISBN: 0 9590735 1 5; 1986, 1989, 1992; 99pp; softcover: AUS $16.99. [Cassettes available from The Language Centre, University of Sydney NSW 2006, Australia.]

• *Readings in Modern Chinese*. Compiled by Liu Wei-ping, Mabel Lee, A. J. Prince, Lily Shaw Lee and R. S. W. Hsu; ISBN: 0 9590735 4 X; 161pp; 1988, 1990, 1992; softcover: AUS $30.00. [Cassettes available from The Language Centre, University of Sydney NSW 2006, Australia]

www.ingramcontent.com/pod-product-compliance
Lightning Source LLC
Chambersburg PA
CBHW080550230426
43663CB00015B/2786